# An Anthology of Essays on Apostolic Leadership

Dr. Joseph Mattera

**Independent self-publishing platform
Createspace**

**Copyright © 2014**

**www.createspace.com**

ISBN 978-1505347531

# TABLE OF CONTENTS

## INTRODUCTION

The following is a collection of essays I have written the past decade on the apostolic. Although I use the term "apostle" quite often, I am mostly referring to it as a function. I do not intend to convey the thought that I think all effective leaders have to use the title apostle or that every great leader is an apostle. I believe true apostolic leaders are few and far between and they are also vastly different from one another.

May this anthology of essays help bring further understanding to the global apostolic movement and may it help advance God's will on the earth.

# CHAPTER 1

## TWELVE CHARACTERISTICS OF THE NEW
## APOSTOLIC LEADERS

The Apostolic Reformation since the mid 90's
signaled the end of identifying Christian movements
merely by denominations. With that, there was a new
emphasis on visionary leaders in the body of Christ
known to function with the five-fold ministry gift of
apostle (Ephesians 4:11).

These apostolic leaders have had a demand upon
them to evolve and improve in regards to best
practices, emotional maturity and leadership style.
The following are twelve of the characteristics of the
new apostolic profile:

### 1. They integrate the message of integrity with the message of kingdom influence

These new apostolic leaders should celebrate the
Christ-like characteristics of simplicity, humility and
personal transformation, not merely cultural

engagement and societal transformation. In light of the leadership scandals of the past three decades, they realize that we cannot have the latter without the former.

## 2. They will need to be ecumenical and collaborate with the church

They should not espouse the old-world Protestant or Catholic divide. The cultural wars against religious freedom have forced the body of Christ to come together and these leaders are amongst those advocating for greater collaboration between different expressions of the church without compromising their distinct theological beliefs. This collaboration also includes forging new partnerships with intentional ethnic diversity.

## 3. They do not focus on ecclesial titles

Unlike many of the leaders in the past, these new apostolic leaders do not depend upon the title of "apostle" or any other ecclesial title to validate or identify their ministry. They believe the fruit of their ministry and influence speaks louder than mere titles.

## 4. They espouse apostolic government with an egalitarian spirit

The book of Acts and the epistles clearly give models of local churches that are under the oversight of apostolic leadership. However, a closer reading of these narratives reveals New Testament apostles urged church leaders to adopt an egalitarian approach replete with a servant's heart, humility and self-sacrifice. A top-down autocratic leadership approach in which apostles impose their will on the congregations was not the biblical norm. Even in a crisis Paul pleaded with the leaders to do the right thing and remove the immoral person among them (1 Cor. 5).

Jesus said that the Roman leadership approach of lording it over their subjects was not the way of the kingdom (Mark 10:42-45). He said that the greatest leaders are the ones who serve. The new rise of apostolic leaders will need to move more away from the heavy-handed style of past generations to more of an egalitarian approach with a bottom-up strategy that employs teams to accomplish kingdom purposes.

## 5. They identify with both church and marketplace leaders

The new apostolic leader understands that the Kingdom of God engages both marketplace and ecclesial leadership. Consequently, they partner with marketplace leaders with an apostolic call to society who are committed to seeing kingdom influence. (In general, these marketplace leaders do not need any ecclesial titles to be effective.)

For example, the early church leadership of Antioch (Acts 13:1-2) involved a businessman with real estate (Barnabas, refer to Acts 4:36-37) and a politician (Manaen), not just a career religious leader (Paul).

Contemporary apostolic leadership has to be sophisticated enough to understand that ecclesial leadership alone is not enough to bring lasting change to both church and culture.

## 6. They are committed to developing kingdom relationships

The new apostolic leader understands that the Kingdom of God is built upon relationships and not only ministry. Hence, they focus much of their time building into key kingdom relationships through informal settings that encourage the development of friendships.

## 7. They are not event driven but process driven

Many apostolic leaders by and large are weary of conferences. They realize that big events take a lot of money, time and effort but often do not produce lasting fruit. They are more prone to investing their time in smaller but more strategic gatherings that create space for dialogue, fellowship, prayer, and strategy instead of monologues that come with the typical conference format.

**8. They are statesmen that can collaborate with those who disagree with them**

The new apostolic leaders are rooted enough in their calling that they are able to integrate on a high level with those of other faiths, ideological and political persuasions, from both the left and the right. They are not stuck in a Christian ghetto where everyone thinks and talks the same. They realize that the world needs their influence and leadership if it will have a chance to experience the kingdom. These leaders function as the salt of the earth and the light of the world.

**9. They are comfortable with both secular and sacred vernacular**

The new apostolic leader is just as conversant with the lingua franca of the secular world as they are the church world. They not only study the Bible but news sources like the Wall Street Journal, the New York Times, the Economist, etc. so they can understand the secular world that most influential people live in. The apostolic leader of the present and future will be just as comfortable speaking with the CEO of a Fortune 500 company as they would be speaking with an ecclesial leader.

## 10. They are entrepreneurs with a kingdom agenda rather than a consumerist agenda

The new apostolic leader will be creative enough to be financially prosperous but holy enough to steward their resources for the sake of the kingdom. Instead of leveraging their wealth for opulent lifestyles they live reasonably and responsibly in the fear of the Lord.

## 11. They have a broader view of cultural engagement than the previous generation

The early 20th century saw the shift from the fundamentalist movement of non-cultural engagement to the evangelical movement of the Christian right with political engagement. The new apostolic leader will have broad interests involving the proper stewardship of creation, human rights, empowering the poor, creating NGOs that serve communities, educational strategies, global initiatives to aid developing nations, micro-financing, sustainable economic policies for nations, and efforts at reconciliation between warring factions. These will not trump, but be in addition to, their engagement regarding religious liberty, marriage, and the sanctity of life.

## 12. They are focused on equipping the next generation

The new apostolic leader will have a multi-generational approach that equips younger leaders to be more effective than the previous generation. This includes intentionally integrating young leaders into their decision-making process, as well as major ministry initiatives. This also involves creating opportunity for them to be creative, to make mistakes and grow as well as preparing them to lead in the marketplace and/or to develop their own networks or organizations.

## CHAPTER 2

## CONTRASTING CHURCH APOSTLES FROM

## APOSTLES OF CHRIST

In 2013 I heard a great prophetic teacher (Thamo Naidoo from South Africa) mention in his message that there is a difference between apostles of churches and apostles of Christ. He said that while there were many apostles of churches, there were only very few true apostles of Christ on the earth today. That one statement exploded on the inside of me and gave me much illumination. I had never heard anyone make this delineation before, but it makes a lot of sense to me. The following is what I have unpacked in the scriptures since Thamo made this statement.

Essentially, the word apostle means a person who is sent to represent another, whether a king, kingdom or entity like a church. First Corinthians 12:28 teaches that God places first in the church apostles, since they are sent by God to represent Him in a city to pioneer a beachhead (a church or ekklesia as shown in Matthew 16:18-19) for city transformation.

Apostles are the "sent ones" who represent the essence of what the church vision or mission is all about. In John 17, Jesus constantly referred to the fact that He was sent by the Father to the world, which is one reason why Hebrews 3:1 refers to Jesus as our Apostle. Jesus was God's Apostle sent into the world to redeem it. In Revelation 22:14 we see the term "the twelve apostles of the Lamb". There will never be another apostle added to that list since there were only twelve. However, it seems evident (at least to me) that Paul was also an apostle of Christ, which means this general category was not limited to merely twelve in total. Paul qualified his apostleship not only by planting churches but also by seeing Jesus (1 Cor. 9:1), which means that apostles at this level must have experienced a dynamic encounter and intimate walk with the Lord.

In the New Testament there were dozens of people identified as apostles. It is my view that since Paul was an apostle of Christ his apostleship transcended the churches he founded. Although Paul did not found the church in Rome, he was respected enough by the general body of Christ that he was able to write the letter to the Romans with apostolic weight and authority as if he was the one who planted it. Hence, apostles of Christ garner a high level of respect beyond the borders of their own church networks, even though they would never attempt to supplant the authority of an apostolic leader who is the founder and/or leader of another network (unless there was heresy or a gross violation of biblical ethics).

Also, Paul warned that there were some who were masquerading as apostles of Christ (2 Cor. 11:13), which probably means that this term (apostle of Christ) was used to identify some significant apostles who were not one of the original twelve.

Furthermore, in 2 Cor. 8:23 Paul identified some as "apostles of the churches" (not "apostles of Christ") which I believe refers to the fact that these leaders only had limited recognized apostolic authority related to representing a particular constellation of churches. Since apostles of Christ directly represent the Lord Jesus, they have a burden and calling for the whole body of Christ and/or a large expression of the global body of Christ. Apostles of Christ are also trans-cultural, trans-generational, and are more loyal to the kingdom of God than to a specific geopolitical affinity.

**The following are ten characteristics of apostles of Christ:**

**1. Apostles of Christ Build the Kingdom**

Oftentimes, church apostles are just focused on their local church and/or their network or denomination. One of the reasons is because their assignment is limited to those works they personally oversee or have founded. They do not have the grace or leadership capacity to go beyond their particular church system, doctrine and/or culture. On the other hand, apostles of Christ have an ambassadorial call that transcends any one church, movement or denomination. Hence, even if they try to focus on one group or movement, God will constantly pull them into other church communities and/or nations to build apostolic foundations related to doctrine or kingdom life.

## 2. Apostles of Christ Are Not Hierarchical

Generally speaking, church apostles can be caught up in titles, measures of influence within their movement, and/or church politics. Apostles of Christ do not personally crave titles (they will use them when appropriate) and do not need institutional church structures to validate their ministry or calling. Of course, true apostles are validated and proven through the grid of the local church.

### 3. Apostles of Christ Don't Strive For Recognition

Philippians 2 teaches us that Jesus made Himself of no reputation. Apostles of Christ are often hidden and do not seek public attention, since they are already rooted strongly in their identity as sons of God and have no innate need for public acclaim.

### 4. Apostles of Christ Are Not Driven by Money

Apostles of Christ have so much faith in their assignment from God, they trust God will provide all their needs as long as they are in His will. They do not go to a place to minister only because the offerings are good but will go only where the Lord is leading. Paul said he did not peddle the word of God for money (2 Cor. 2:17) and the apostle Peter warns shepherds not to minister for dishonest gain (1 Peter 5:2). Although I believe those who labor in the word full-time are worthy of double honor and should make a living from the gospel (1 Tim. 5:17; 1 Cor. 9:14), the bottom line for apostles of Christ is the will of God, not material gain.

## 5. Apostles of Christ Lay Down their Lives for the Gospel

All of the original twelve apostles (except John) as well as the apostle Paul were martyred for the gospel. As Jesus laid down His life for the sheep (John 10) those who represent Him are willing to die daily (Revelation 12:11; Acts 20:24; Galatians 2:19-20) whether it is to their own will or to literally lose their lives.

## 6. Apostles of Christ Have a Servant's Heart

Apostles of Christ are unassuming, do not have an entitlement mentality, have a servant's heart, and do not lead with a top-down autocratic approach like the rulers of the Gentiles (Mark 10:42). They mimic Jesus' words when He said that the greatest in the Kingdom is the one who serves (Mark 10:43-45).

## 7. Apostles of Christ Have Divine Influence and Calling Beyond their Network of Churches

Although the apostle Paul strove not to preach where Christ was already named (Romans 15:20) his greatest epistle was to the church at Rome, where he endeavored to go in spite of the fact he was not their founding apostle. Paul had vast influence way beyond the primary sphere of activity he was focusing on (Read 2 Corinthians 10:10-14). His influence has even reached to us 2,000 years later through his inspired New Testament writings.

Since apostles of Christ represent the Lord Himself, by nature they have to be trans-national, trans-cultural, and multi-generational and have a desire for kingdom advancement, not just the enlargement of their church networks.

## 8. Apostles of Christ Have an Intimate Walk with God

Since apostles of Christ have to represent Jesus and not merely a church or denomination (of course all believers are called to represent Christ but apostolic callings have a greater measure of responsibility), they are obligated to know God intimately and walk in His presence and power. All of the original twelve apostles walked with Jesus personally for more than three years before they were launched into their ministry, and Paul the apostle had a personal encounter with Jesus on the road to Damascus (Acts 9). All true apostles of Christ will have a driving passion to know God and to make Him known.

**9. Apostles of Christ Endure Great Hardship**

Paul validated his apostleship by the immense hardships he endured, not just by signs and wonders and church planting (2 Corinthians 11:17-12:8). Paul said (1 Cor. 4:9) that apostles live like those who are condemned to die in the arena (have the sentence of death upon themselves). This kind of apostolic leader must have the capacity for high-stress leadership combined with the kind of emotional maturity to deal with all kinds of difficulties that the average person could never endure.

**10. Apostles of Christ Live in Simplicity**

Apostles of Christ do not need or desire to live a life of extreme luxury and opulence. Their spiritual and psychological needs are constantly nurtured through their deep and abiding relationship with Christ. They have been so satisfied with living with the person and presence of God that they count all things as dung compared to knowing Him (Philippians 3:8-14). Their greatest desire in life is to fellowship with Him, meditate on the scriptures, and serve God's people and kingdom. Consequently they do not need to drive the most expensive cars, live in the largest houses or make a huge salary in order to be satisfied in this life. Consequently, they live in simplicity, are content with much or with little and are not driven to pursue material possessions and pleasure. (This is not to say having things is wrong or sinful)

After seeing these 10 traits, we can see how there are only very few apostles of Christ in this world. May the Lord raise more up in these days so the body of Christ can fully advance.

# CHAPTER 3

## APOSTOLIC KEYS FOR ACTIVATION AND IMPLEMENTATION FROM NEHEMIAH

The book of Nehemiah is an outstanding book for going from a compelling vision to its activation and implementation. Nehemiah was a type of a master builder apostle (1 Corinthians 3:10-14) who knew how to utilize teams, motivate the masses, and bring commitment through conviction. His leadership ability resulted in the rebuilding of the walls of Jerusalem and his methods are replicable.

**The following are some of the key apostolic principles he used:**

**1. He assessed the true conditions of his people and nation (Nehemiah 1:1-3)**

Many people are delusional or in denial regarding the true state of their nation, church and community. Leadership involves bringing self-awareness to those under their care and influence. Without knowing the truth there can never be a path to true freedom (John 8:32-46).

## 2. He was moved inwardly and received a compelling vision to meet the need (1:4)

All leadership is driven and motivated by vision. All true vision must emanate from the heart and have passion. Vision merely articulated via strategy on paper is never enough. Spirit-inspired passion is the engine that drives heaven-sent vision.

## 3. He prayed his vision through before he attempted to implement it (1:4-11)

Godly leadership is a partnership with the divine since we are living both on the earth and in heavenly places (Ephesians 2:4-6). Like Nehemiah, leaders must pray their vision through in the Spirit before attempting to implement it in the natural.

Without consistent seasons of individual and corporate prayer, vision will fail because the spiritual warfare and natural circumstances of this world will offer too much resistance without giving God opportunity to speak and to move.

**4. He gathered all the human resources he needed based on his relationships (1:11--he was cupbearer to the king)**

Successful leaders pull on all their relationships to gather the supplies and connections needed to implement their vision. Everyone has a constellation of relationships and within that circle is usually the provision for the vision. Instead of always looking on the outside for your answers, most of the time the people and resources you need to fulfill your vision are already in your midst.

**5. He succinctly articulated his compelling vision in a few sentences (2:17-18)**

All vision and mission should be collapsed down to brief mottos, acronyms or statements that easily describe the vision and motivate the people. Vision and/or mission statements that are too long or convoluted make it difficult for the average person to wrap their brain around it and understand it. God told Habakkuk to write the vision down and make it plain so that the messenger could run with it (Hab. 2:2).

Hence, every person in an organization or congregation should be able to convey the vision of the house. Consequently, when people do not have the vision or know the vision they are scattered and aimless (Proverbs 29:18).

## 6. He refused to be distracted by opposition (2:19-20; 6:2-4)

Every leader and organization will have to contend with competing voices and loyalties that demand focus and attention. One of the great keys to the vision is to be able to stay focused and keep the main thing the main thing, and keep first things first. If Satan cannot destroy you he will try to distract you with good or appealing things that can lure you away from God's best plan for your life. (Satan doesn't come in a red suit and pitchfork but appears as an

angel of light according to 2 Corinthians 11:14.)

**7. He utilized a team of volunteers committed to**

**the cause (3:1-32)**

No growing organization can survive if it depends

merely upon a few people. Every successful vision

requires a team of committed people to fulfill the

dream. For example, the two model churches of the

New Testament (in Jerusalem and Antioch) both had

a great team of leaders and layers of other leaders

who worked together.

**8. He instilled courage during times of testing**

**(4:8-12, 14)**

There will always be opposition, high stress, drama,

unforeseen events and crises that oppose godly

vision. Leaders have to remain calm, speak peace,

have courage and continue to function with high

capacity during times of stress, duress and testing.

If you want a church or organization without stress

or spiritual warfare then ask God to take you home to

heaven right now. (That's the only place where there is no more crying, sorrow or pain.)

## 9. He set up systems of communication to unite all for battle (4:13, 16-22)

The people were not only committed to their vision, but were committed to protecting and advancing their vision. To fulfill vision, every person has to be trained for battle and be mobilized instantly when an attack comes that threatens the vision. Every church especially needs intercessors in place who can be contacted instantly and all leaders need to be able to mobilize for strategy with little notice.

## 10. The people were all bound together with a written covenant (9:38; 13:1-31)

People need to be bound together by a written covenant that lays out everything expected. Whatever people don't sign on to, they will not be accountable to.

Generally, people don't do what you expect; they do what you inspect. Nehemiah had to follow up on the covenant by inspecting and enforcing the application of the covenant in chapter 13.

Leaders are not primarily called to be your friends they are called to push you, hold you accountable and to challenge your complacency if you are not growing.

## 11. The leaders were all committed to living in the place of their mission (11:1-2)

Nehemiah made all the leaders live within the walls of Jerusalem even though it was dangerous. Leaders are called to live in the community they are ministering to so that they have the same care and concern for the wellbeing of the people they live amongst. Nehemiah celebrated all those who lived in the community and sent ten percent of the people to live there.

I have been living in proximity to the community and city I was called to since 1980 even though many of my friends have larger houses with much property outside our city region. I believe Nehemiah demonstrates that our goal should not be comfort but conforming to the will of God in our lives.

## 12. He was a great fundraiser for the house of God (13:10-12)

Without provision, the vision is only a dream and will never be a reality. All successful leaders have to be successful fundraisers! The apostle Paul only wrote one chapter devoted to love (1 Cor. 13) but wrote two whole chapters devoted to fundraising for his ministry (2 Cor. 8-9).

Furthermore, I believe every church should have enough in tithes and offerings so that the lead pastor does not have to work outside the church, this way their time is not divided and they are not too tired to serve the congregation.

Finally, there is much more in this incredible book that God gave us to teach the principles of organization, teamwork and city building. Nehemiah illustrates that preaching the word isn't enough for community transformation.  If that were the case then all he needed was to let Ezra the biblical scribe do his thing and it would have happened automatically. No, we need to have a partnership between marketplace and full-time church leaders for city building.

# CHAPTER 4

## WERE YOU "SENT" OR JUST "WENT" INTO MINISTRY?

Today there are many people in the independent Evangelical and Pentecostal movements who start churches merely because they feel led to do so.

If there were a way to statistically track the outcomes of these self-ordained pastors, my educated guess, based on years of experience, is that most of these churches and/or ministries fail to last more than a few years.

In our American culture we glorify independence and self-determination. These values are great when it comes to our entrepreneurial spirit, which is why our nation will probably always take the lead in creativity and wealth creation and our economy will continue to rebound in spite of what the federal government does to us. But when it comes to functioning properly in the body of Christ these values can be harmful.

Unfortunately, the way many of our brothers and sisters have "called themselves" to start churches or launch ministries mimics Hollywood movies more than biblical protocol! I am thinking of movies that depict independent fundamentalist evangelicals like "The Apostle" (staring Robert Duvall) and "Elmer Gantry" (staring Burt Lancaster). The former highlights a man who baptizes himself and calls himself an apostle, while the latter features a man who conducts tent crusades without any ministerial training or affiliation to a church, association, or denomination.

A telling scene in "Elmer Gantry" involves a group of pastors and a newspaper reporter asking evangelist Elmer Gantry and a lady evangelist a simple question: Who trained and ordained you? Their response: "God" did.

These movies demonstrate that even secularists understand there is something wrong with this way of doing ministry. It is as ridiculous as sending yourself to Afghanistan to fight Islamic terrorists without the covering, protection, training, or the strategy of the U.S. military. I have had experiences in my own church in which a person left the church without proper training, communication, or protocol with plans to start a church elsewhere. My primary question to people such as these is "Who sent you?"

I tell our church members that when they meet a minister or pastor for the first time, one of the first things they need to inquire about is who sent them and who are they accountable to? If the minister or pastor has no one they answer to then run from them as fast as you can. Many have started local churches for the same reason some entrepreneurs start their own small businesses instead of working for a larger company: they simply don't want to submit to anyone else or have someone over them telling them what to do.

One of the greatest chapters in the Bible is the priestly prayer of Jesus in John 17 in which Jesus is praying to the Father before His crucifixion. In this prayer Jesus constantly refers to the fact that He was "sent" or "given" things to Him by His Father to do the work He gave Him to do. This shows He never called Himself to minister; Jesus needed to be sent or given ministry by someone higher than Himself for His ministry to be legitimate, even though He is God the Son (John 17:2-4, 6-9, 11-12, 18, 21, 23-25).

If the Son of God didn't call Himself into ministry then others who feel called ought to pattern themselves after His protocol for confirming the timing of a genuine call into ministry. Furthermore, the Bible tells us in Hebrews 5:1, 3-6 that Jesus didn't call Himself into the priesthood; he waited until the Father called Him. This was patterned after the Old Covenant in which a person could only serve as a priest if his physical father was a priest of the tribe of Levi from the priestly line of Aaron (Exodus 28:1). Thus, if we don't have a father who ordained us into the ministry (in the New Covenant this includes spiritual fathers) then we have a "bastard" ministry and have no biblical legitimacy to fulfill our calling.

The early church also functioned with this concept of sending as a methodological background. For example, even though Saul and Barnabas had already felt called by God into ministry they didn't dare send themselves until the leaders of the church in Antioch also received a confirming word from the Lord to send them. (Read Acts 13:1-2, in which the tense of the original Greek wording shows that God had already called Saul into the ministry before the leaders of the church received the confirming word.)

In another instance, Paul the apostle submitted the gospel of grace he was preaching (to the Gentiles) to the leading apostles of the Jerusalem Church (Peter and John) for fear his work was in vain (Galatians 2:2,

9). This shows even Paul, the great apostle, needed the right hand of apostolic blessing to be considered legitimate.

Paul also shows it was part of the protocol of the early church that a person wouldn't preach or minister unless they were officially sent and, by implication, sanctioned by the church. (Read Romans 10:15 which says "How shall they preach unless they are sent?")

In spite of this biblical precedent, many ministers I meet have started their churches from no more than a subjective "leading of the Lord" without the training, blessing, or sending of a local church body. If a person cannot go through the grid of submitting to a process of biblical training, character development, and theological and ministerial training in the context of a local church, then how can they be properly prepared to shepherd a flock under God? Most of the time when someone has no personal submission to spiritual authority it illustrates a deeper issue within them of rebellion against God! Jesus said that if we receive the one He sent then we receive Him. Conversely, by rejecting the spiritual authority He sent then we reject Him (Mathew 10:40).

I have experienced everything I have written in this article the hard way. For example, when I first received a calling from the Lord to enter full-time ministry (in October 1980) the first thing I did was submit my revelation to my pastor, Benjamin Crandall. Even though I felt called to start a church I submitted to his counsel which included sitting under his tutelage for several years until he licensed me for ministry. It was four whole years of preaching in my community before he finally came to me and told me it was time to start a church, which I did in 1984. I believe that, because I submitted to his spiritual authority as my spiritual father, our church has been blessed with having no church splits in 31 years and unity amongst all of our elders and pastors. Also, I sense a special anointing and grace upon me to teach on spiritual authority and church government. Conversely, some I know who started churches about the same time as me have experienced multiple church splits because they didn't submit to the biblical process involved in a ministerial calling. This includes training, ordination, and submission to spiritual authority in the context of a local church or ministry.

Furthermore, when some bishops in my city approached me in 2005 about consecrating me as a bishop, the first thing I did before allowing such a consecration was to have them call several local and national bishops who knew me well to obtain feedback before we continued. If those leaders didn't agree that I was already functioning as a bishop then I didn't want to proceed! (They received confirmation from several bishops which then began a one-year process in which I submitted to a rigorous grid in which they interviewed apostolic leaders, my elders, and my family to verify the legitimacy of my calling as a bishop.)

In spite of the above, I believe there are exceptions to these protocols especially in certain places in the world where there are no local churches or apostolic leaders, or where there are no spiritual fathers willing to process and release younger ministers into the ministry. But, in this nation it is very easy to find someone willing to mentor, train, and release a person into the ministry.

The first place to look is in your own local church. Most times there is a biblical process that is either structured or informal that a person can go through to be sent out into full-time church ministry. However, if you want to start a church, you should first prove yourself by either running a successful home group that rapidly multiplies or oversee a ministry in your local church that successfully nurtures and trains leaders. If you cannot prove your pastoral calling with the blessing of a senior pastor in your local church then that is a good sign you will not

be successful as the founding pastor of a new local

church.

# CHAPTER 5

## CONTRASTS BETWEEN THE APOSTOLIC CHURCH AND THE CONTEMPORARY CHURCH

There has been a movement the past four decades amongst various segments of the body of Christ towards embracing the way of Jesus and the apostles as found in the first century church. Extensive writing has been done in this regard by Jeff Reed, the founder of BILD International (www.bild.org) who has given his life over to writing about the Pauline model of church multiplication and leadership development. Most recently, Dr. C. Peter Wagner has started a network of leaders who have been launching a movement of apostolic centers in the United States and beyond! (Peter has a knack for sensing what is practically needed and then galvanizing a movement around it.)

This movement is very necessary since the contemporary and traditional church of the past centuries (perhaps since the 2nd and 3rd centuries) has in some ways lost its sense of apostolicity! Regarding the contemporary church, essentially the focus of the congregation and pastor is only to build up their local congregation and serve their community. If they have a vision for missions they generally will support "full-time missionaries" that may or may not have had their genesis in their congregation. Furthermore, if a local congregation has a vision to serve beyond their traditional local church functions, they will likely partner with a parachurch organization that specializes in marketplace ministry, soul winning, or community transformation (often disconnecting extra-local ministry from the discipleship process and life of their congregation).

Generally speaking, the typical contemporary local congregation has no vision beyond the care and concern for their own flock and adding to their membership. Even if a church has an apostolic vision to release fivefold ministers (Ephesians 4:11) to serve the greater body of Christ, most of the time they send out the founding apostle and have very little connection to him. Consequently, the church often becomes autonomous from outside interference and/or apostolic governance.

## The New Testament Model for Apostolic Churches/Centers

As we read the New Testament, we see that every city had one church (that met in many locations in house church congregations) that was led by an apostle who founded this city church. The apostle would nurture and raise up elders and shepherds who would care for the flock (Acts 14:22-23; 15:36; 20:28) and then leave and start other churches and then periodically return to make sure they remained true to the faith. Paul the Apostle was sent out of the church of Antioch (Acts 13:1-2) and then started other churches that he continued to oversee as the founding apostle, even though he was not present.

Thus, the modus operandi of the first century church was as follows: an apostle would found a congregation, stay long enough to nurture elders, and then the apostle would leave that city to found another citywide movement of congregations but continue to revisit each of these churches and give them guidance and oversee them, but of course from a macro level.

In summary, though Paul's ministry didn't remain in the cities of Ephesus, Colossae, Philippi, Thessalonica and Crete, his governance as the founding apostle continued on through the elders and leaders he set in each church. This clearly demonstrates that in apostolic churches (or centers), ministry location and focus is not necessary for (apostolic) governance.

Paul left the elders to deal with the various issues related to the congregation but when it came to the doctrine, teaching and standards of the congregations he had the final say. In Corinth, he even threatened the leaders and congregation and said to them "what do you prefer, shall I come to you with a rod of discipline or shall I come in love and with a gentle spirit?" (1 Corinthians 5:23) He goes on to give orders to put an unrepentant sexually immoral person out of the church (1 Corinthians 5:12) as well as guidelines on who church members were able to associate with (1 Corinthians 5).

Furthermore, the whole epistle to the Galatians is a doctrinal defense of his apostleship to that city church as well as setting them straight regarding the gospel they were preaching; the epistle to the Ephesians contains commandments on how the church family was expected to function (chapters 4-6); in the epistle to the Philippians, Paul urges the leaders to work together in unity (4:2-3); in 1 Timothy 3 and Titus 1, Paul gives instructions regarding the criteria for elders and deacons. In some instances Paul pled with the leaders to do things correctly and in other instances he just gave out apostolic orders and/or commands that were not up for negotiation. Hence, apostolic leadership generally tries to empower the local eldership to lead the church and only gets involved in matters regarding breaches of doctrine, ethics, and protocol.

Not only this, but every one of the churches Paul started had a commitment to continue their partnership with Paul as the founder by financially supporting his apostolic ministry (read Philippians 1:5, 18-19; 2 Corinthians 8-9).

Many of these congregations also supplied people who would serve alongside Paul on his apostolic team (Philippians 1:25-30; 2 Corinthians 8:16-24; Romans 16:1-2).

In summary, the first century apostolic church had the following as a general template:

- A leader was sent out of the city church as an apostle

- The apostle would plant other churches in other cities
- In each church the apostle would leave and plant another church after a strong eldership team was raised up to care for the flock
- These churches had a global apostolic vision by continuing to stay connected to their apostle with financial support, praying regularly for him, supplying co-workers for the apostolic team, and by staying accountable and keeping regular communication with him
- The apostle continued to have governmental rule without ministerial proximity and hands-on leadership.

**Apostolic Centers**

The present movement of apostolic centers has continued to build upon this first century model as stated above and is attempting to create (long needed) change in the way we in the United States typically do church. Some in the movement don't like to use the word "elders" because they say this word is not mentioned in the New Testament while the founding apostle is present. I think this point is moot since Peter calls himself an elder (1 Peter 5:1). Hence, even when the founding apostolic team is present in a local church they are all essentially biblical elders. They use the term "centers" rather than churches perhaps to disassociate themselves from the baggage of the present day church. Also, with the restoration of the teaching of the Kingdom of God in the present day apostolic reformation, many (apostolic leaders) in this movement have conceptually gone from overseeing an inbred congregation that exists merely to care for itself to having a center replete with kingdom activity that encourages and equips their members and leaders to reach every cultural mountain of society. (I personally continue to use the words "elders" and "churches" because those are the words used by the New Testament writers but calling an influential congregation a "center" may be a wise move in various contexts.)

Furthermore, I am excited about this new development since our local church (Resurrection Church of New York) has always called itself an apostolic church. Our church has had major influence in our Sunset Park community in Brooklyn (of about 180,000) and has modeled the apostolic church of the New Testament since we founded it in 1984. For the past two decades we have had all five of the ministry gifts functioning amongst our leadership, and we have been an equipping center that has sent out numerous church leaders and nurtured influential marketplace leaders that have served our region and beyond. Also, as part of the apostolic cycle mentioned above, I have launched out apostolically to the nations while still remaining as the apostolic overseer. Since 1990 I have been able to function apostolically to our city and now to numerous cities because we have had a strong leadership team in place that cared for our congregation without losing our kingdom focus.

Finally, the Reformation that started in 1517 with Martin Luther continues on as the reformed church continues to reform itself.

# CHAPTER 6

## TWELVE DIFFERENT KINDS OF APOSTOLIC LEADERS

I have been in the apostolic movement since the late 1980's and have observed many kinds of apostolic leaders. By "apostolic" I am referring to a person who functions in the apostolic ministry gift as mentioned in Ephesians 4:11. They may also oversee an apostolic church that exerts great influence in their community, and/or lead a network of churches.

One size definitely doesn't fit all in the apostolic, or in any of the other ministry gifts for that matter! They all have different modes of operation and/or function as well as different motivational gifts and bents. Of course, any true apostolic leader may have one or more of the following characteristics.

The following are the different kinds of apostolic leaders I have observed:

## 1. The Connecting Apostle

These apostolic leaders are like the Apostle Barnabas mentioned in the Book of Acts. Barnabas was always connecting people together and was the one responsible for connecting Saul (later on he became the great Apostle Paul) to the Jerusalem church (Acts 9:26-27). These leaders love networking key people together, function with a strong heart of mercy (they give people second and third chances; read Acts 15:37-39), and have an amazing understanding of where to place people for the maximization of their gifts and callings.

This kind of leader also has a burden for unifying the Body of Christ and are adept at creating horizontal networks or associations of leaders in their regions, either for fellowship or to fulfill a joint mission (hence they are usually quite ecumenical).

## 2. The Truth Apostle

Paul the Apostle focused on teaching the truth and was committed to maturing people in the faith through his teaching ministry (Colossians 1:24-29). These are scholarly leaders who write much and attract people into their networks of influence through their great scholarship and practical insight. They also major on quality, doctrine and developing covenantal systems of engagement within their circles of influence.

What separates these from others with mere theological theory is their ability to form strong coalitions with high-level commitment to advance the kingdom mandate of spreading the gospel.

## 3. The Prophetic Apostle

These are intuitive leaders who have an amazing ability to think quickly with words of wisdom from the Lord. They are great visionaries and dreamers and think ahead of the curve and have a great gift of exhortation and/or preaching extemporaneously.

With their great gift of motivation, they are able to attract many leaders into their spheres of influence.

**4. The Military Apostle**

These are like military generals in the Body of Christ who create hierarchical networks with a strong top-down leadership approach. They usually lead strong vertical networks with high commitment and are not really interested in participating in ecumenical associations (unless it fits their particular agenda or they lead it). This is because they are so focused on their purpose and lack patience and grace to work with other strong leaders who have a different view of the church or who do not want to submit to their leadership.

**5. The Cultural Apostle**

These apostolic leaders attract leaders into their networks because of political/social issues and causes such as social justice and the like. They have a prophetic bent and are also great unifiers of like-minded leaders.

## 6. The Signs and Wonders Apostle

These apostolic leaders are like the Apostle Peter who spread the gospel by the use of extraordinary signs and wonders through the gift of faith (Acts 5:15). These leaders can draw great crowds, build large churches, and regularly take risks of faith regarding finances, building bigger buildings, as well as helping others walk in the supernatural. They will draw other pastors and leaders into their networks who are hungry for the supernatural.

## 7. The Community Apostle

These apostolic leaders dive into the economic, social and political lives of their communities with a goal of shepherding their cities, not just a congregation. Many of these leaders create programs that serve their communities with their churches or networks that become key agents of change for surrounding areas.

## 8. The Missiological Apostle

This apostolic leader is focused on statistics, trends, demographics and cultural relevance, and helps lead innovative networks and/or organizations that lead the global charge to spread the gospel. They are very scholarly and introspective yet brilliant leaders who are totally focused upon kingdom expansion for the glory of God. They are great lecturers in conferences and provide a great service for the Body of Christ at large as they, like the sons of Issachar (1 Chron. 12:32), understand the times and know what the church ought to do.

## 9. The Shepherding Apostle

This is an apostolic leader who is more focused upon the lives of the leaders of their network than upon having a corporate mission. They have a paternal anointing and take the most joy in washing the feet of their sons and daughters so they fulfill their vision and destiny! This is perhaps the most lacking apostolic leader in the church today since there is a dearth in the church regarding true apostolic spiritual parenting.

## 10. The Entrepreneurial Apostle

This kind of apostolic leader is a hyphenated leader with a dual ministry of church and business who creates wealth through initiatives that support the work of the Kingdom of God. This kind of entrepreneurial ability attracts many leaders who desire an impartation from them so they can also be prosperous in everything they touch!

## 11. The Statesman Apostle

This kind of apostolic leader is a very wise person who is able to represent the Kingdom of God to other denominations and those in the political and social realms. They are generally very ecumenical and have a ministry of reconciliation and are sometimes called upon to be peacemakers between opposing groups. These leaders are usually respected by Christian and non-Christian alike and are by nature very ecumenical.

## 12. The Intercessory Apostle

These apostolic leaders spend much time in prayer and engage in high-level spiritual warfare so light can break through in dark places. They are able to attract enough people to start large organized networks of pastors and leaders who believe their main calling is to expand the kingdom through prayer and spiritual warfare strategies. What separates these from typical prophetic intercessors is that they not only have a great gift of prayer but also are able to create influential networks of prayer leaders.

In closing, many leaders I know probably stand in about three to four of the categories above. These twelve kinds were written for the sake of clarity but not meant to legalistically confine our thinking in such a way that limits our perspective regarding apostolic leadership. Also, there are probably many other categories others could think of, which would further complicate and mesh various anointing and ministry functions together.

## CHAPTER 7

## THE APOSTOLIC VERSUS THE PASTORAL

## PREACHING MODEL

The word of God teaches us that those set in to minister to the body of Christ have a function based on their supernatural and motivational giftings. How someone is "wired" will determine how they view life, the church, the priorities of Christianity, and ministry.

I have noticed through the years a difference between those who emphasize ministerial responsibilities and tasks (human doing) from those who emphasize emotional health and internal piety (human "being") as priorities in the Christian walk; both are needed. This emphasis will be based on whether the person doing the teaching has more of an apostolic perspective (based on the old Roman usage of the term, which has to do with Rome sending a military leader called an apostle to another nation to form a beachhead for the purpose of conquering it for Rome) or a pastoral perspective (a person whose primary concern is nurture and personal wellbeing). Understanding these two viewpoints will greatly aid us in critiquing books and teachings and also help us to know what our church or organization may need at the present time.

Sometimes we need to be nurtured and cared for before we go out to minister; sometimes we need to be in the battle advancing the cause of Christ. We want to avoid falling into one extreme or the other by reading books from both these camps and allowing both types to speak into our lives.

The following are general principles (some are overstatements) regarding the two perspectives.

- Pastoral preaching is therapeutic; Apostolic preaching emphasizes personal commitment in spite of how we feel.
- Pastoral preaching emphasizes inward health; Apostolic preaching emphasizes external tasks.

- Pastoral preaching emphasizes our call to understand our true self by contemplation; Apostolic preaching emphasizes our commission to make God known by cultural penetration.

- Pastoral preaching is essential for a healthy church; Apostolic preaching is necessary for a Christ-centered city.

- Pastoral preaching aids us in self-discovery and recovery; Apostolic preaching promotes societal transformation that can lead to the restoration of God's kingdom principles on earth as in heaven.

- Pastoral preaching emphasizes relational stability for the communion of the saints; Apostolic preaching assembles the saints in purposeful unity to fulfill the Great Commission.

- Pastoral preaching emphasizes self-renewal; Apostolic preaching emphasizes personal responsibility.

- Pastoral preaching is inward-focused and promotes counseling strategies for the sheep;

Apostolic preaching is outward-focused and promotes evangelism and making disciples of the nations.

In conclusion:

- The pastor is sent out to counsel; The apostolic leader to conquer.

- Every person needs a pastor; All people groups need an apostle.

- Every pastor needs an apostolic leader; Every apostolic leader needs another one to pastor him or her.

# CHAPTER 8

## ABUSES AND BLESSINGS OF THE CONTEMPORARY APOSTOLIC MOVEMENT

As a person who has been part of the Apostolic Movement since 1989 I have seen the good, the bad and the ugly. That being said, I believe all of the fivefold ministry gifts mentioned in Ephesians 4:11 have always been present throughout church history (leaders were functioning these ways, whether they used these titles or not). Consequently, I have known many leaders who legitimately functioned in apostolic leadership and I have known many who have used the title without apostolic fruit and legitimacy. (For example, I have been blessed to know and work with many outstanding and legitimate apostolic leaders in the Apostolic Reformation such as John Kelly, C. Peter Wagner, Ron Cottle, Bill Hamon, Emanuele Cannistraci, Harry Jackson, Dale Bronner, and all those I serve with on the ICAL council, and many others too numerous to mention in this article, not only in the U.S. but around the world. Go to www.uscal.us for more information on ICAL.)

(By "apostolic leadership" I mean a leader who functions in the ministry gift of apostle as found in Ephesians 4:11.)

As we examine scripture we can say many things about what the signs of an apostle are. But today I am referring to a leader who oversees a network of churches and/or leads a strong apostolic church with much influence in their community.

Furthermore, apostolic churches also tend to meet many practical needs of their communities and send out many homegrown leaders to plant churches as well as send out marketplace leaders to transform society.

**The following are some of the blessings of recognizing apostolic leadership:**

## 1. When we recognize the title we can also more easily release the function

Some who favor the use of the title "apostle" say we need to recognize apostles in the same way we need the military to have uniforms, titles and ranks that release them to their functions. Not having the title will cause confusion in the chain of command as well as among civilians since they will not know who is responsible to enforce the laws of the land and protect them.

## 2. The recognition of the apostolic merely allows for the fivefold ministry designations of the New Testament

Some proponents of using the title "apostle" say the most pure expression of the Body of Christ in church history was the first century church, which recognized the ministry gifts of Ephesians 4:11. If it was good enough for Jesus and the early church it should be necessary for us to do the same if we want the same kind of fruit.

**3. Recognizing the apostolic can also help usher in a new apostolic reformation**

Some proponents of the apostolic say it is evident the old way of doing things through hierarchical denominationalism is dead or dying (with the exception of Pentecostal denominations, like the Assemblies of God, most denominations are on the decline). By recognizing apostolic ministry we could further accelerate the apostolic reformation that is based on the galvanization of voluntary associations of pastors and leaders in regions irrespective of denominational affiliations.

This reformation recognizes visionary leaders in each region that God has anointed to unite the Body of Christ and bring societal change. Often denominational bishops and/or superintendents are just gifted administrators without the leadership capacity to galvanize churches to reach a city or nation. Recognizing apostolic leadership (irrespective of denominational affiliation) can remove this bottleneck and release the authority and power of the Kingdom of God in a city!

## 4. Apostolic networks are amongst the largest movements expanding Christianity in the earth today

As we examine what is happening in Asia, Africa and Latin America we find the greatest expansion of the church today is coming from apostolic leadership and their networks of churches that are producing great movements! Thus the current great global expansion of the church is no longer being led by typical denominations. Even when denominations are involved they are usually cooperating with apostolic visionaries who may or may not belong to a denomination.

## 5. It will help the church expand from local to extra-local because the nature of the apostolic is to establish new territory for God

Typically, pastoral ministry is inwardly focused only on a congregation. Apostolic leadership is always concerned with the expansion of the Kingdom of God. Consequently, when apostolic leadership is recognized and encouraged the church will nurture leadership that not only shepherds congregations but also shepherds communities and cities.

In the early church the apostles only stayed in a local church long enough to establish them with elders and pastors who would care for the church. Then the apostles were financially supported and sent out to establish new churches and reach new territories. Hence, without this apostolic understanding we could greatly limit kingdom expansion.

**Some abuses of the apostolic:**

(By "abuses" I am referring to the misuse of either the title or the position. To be fair, most of these same issues can be used for pastors, bishops in any denomination, and anyone who attempts to use a title or position to leverage power for themselves. However, since I am a part of the apostolic movement, I am focusing on some issues in this movement.)

## 1. Many leaders who use the title have no apostolic fruit

I must admit that, in the 30 years that I have been exposed to apostolic ministry, a large percentage of the leaders who call themselves apostles lack apostolic fruit in their ministry! This shows me these leaders are using the title to artificially grant themselves some sort of prestige. But what they don't realize is they run the risk of making themselves look bad.

For example, almost without exception, all of the legitimate apostolic leaders I know in the New York City region do not call themselves apostles; they just let their fruit speak for them. The more fruit you have, the less you need to use a title amongst the leadership you labor with.

## 2. Many apostolic leaders have an autocratic leadership style

Unfortunately, all too often those who gravitate to the use of a title like "apostle" (I would include "bishop" as well, to be fair) tend to have an autocratic approach with a heavy, top-down leadership style. They are prone to giving out strategies and commands without allowing a team into the decision-making process. Autocrats rarely develop homegrown leaders and often have a hard time cultivating true transparent relationships with their spiritual sons and daughters.

To be fair, I also know many apostolic leaders who have used the title, like Apostle John Kelly and those I serve with on the ICAL Apostolic Council, who are fantastic at leadership placement and developing effective strategies through teams and ad hoc thinktanks. (But, all too often, apostolic leaders are without the mentoring of seasoned apostolic leaders like the aforementioned ICAL council members.)

**3. Many who call themselves apostles have an independent spirit and don't work well with denominational overseers or leaders of evangelical associations**

Since I travel extensively to minister all over the world I have heard several "war stories" involving so-called apostles who think they are above other leaders and arrogantly only support ministry endeavors they themselves initiate and/or lead.

Furthermore, many of them also believe all denominational leaders are old wineskin and disregard and discount them. Just because someone is in the apostolic movement doesn't mean they are favored by God or on the cutting edge above denominational leaders. There are many incredible denominational leaders without the title of "apostle" who have apostolic fruit and anointing!

**4. Some identified in the apostolic movement have caused division in certain nations**

Some apostolic leaders are unwilling to work with other groups and, in their insecurity, have actually caused strife and division rather than unity in the Body of Christ. (Of course, we could say that about every expression of Christianity.) Unfortunately, these few leaders have given the whole movement a reputation of being arrogant opportunists who build their own empires rather than God's kingdom. As a result, there are several nations I go to where I can't even use the word "apostolic" because of all the negative baggage it connotes.

**5. Some in the apostolic are hierarchical and believe they have more God-given authority than the average pastor in their region**

Some have used the title to artificially promote themselves and think that since they are an apostle they automatically have more authority in their region than all other pastors and leaders.

Some have even pronounced they are "the" apostle to their city or nation—a designation a true apostle would shun because it exhibits pride and presumption as well as disrespect towards other key leaders in their region who may have more influence than they do. In cities such as New York there are so many networks, ethnicities and movements that it would be virtually impossible for one person to be truly "the" apostle to the city. Even though I have labored in this city for over 30 years there are still probably key apostolic leaders and networks I have never heard of (and who probably never heard of me!).

Unfortunately, some are so hung up on titles, protocols and hierarchy they lose sight of the nature of Christ and the early apostles, who built upon servant leadership and were anti-hierarchical (read Mark 10:42-45).

**6. Some in the apostolic have taken pastors and churches away from their associations and brought them under their own "covering"**

In my travels I have heard of a few apostolic leaders from the USA who offered poor pastors in developing nations financial aid if they would leave their denominations and join their networks of churches. Behavior like this has caused much suspicion amongst denominational and evangelical leaders. True apostolic leaders never build upon the foundation of other leaders and they definitely never try to build their ministries by bribing or taking vulnerable leaders away from their spiritual overseers (unless there is an ethical reason to leave said overseer).

**7. Many apostles are self-appointed**

(To be fair, many pastors and bishops are self-appointed as well.)

Like the movie The Apostle with Robert Duvall, many hear teaching on the apostolic and appoint themselves or tell the elders of their churches to

appoint them as apostles.

# CHAPTER 9

## TWELVE ESSENTIALS RELATED TO APOSTOLIC TRUTH

There has been much said in recent years regarding the office of apostle and how they should function. Even mainline Evangelical leaders are using the term "apostolic" to describe certain types of leaders. Consequently I feel the need to put together a brief summary of what I want to call "apostolic truth," which is a fancy way of saying what apostolic understanding should include, in my opinion.

To me, apostolic truth is not mere doctrine or concept but is mainly built upon practical experience and action. Apostolic truth that does not involve high risk, accomplishment and action is not truly apostolic.

**The following are what I believe are some of the essential principles of apostolic truth.**

**1. Apostolic truth involves personal and ministerial transparency with high-stress capacity and endurance**

In 2 Corinthians chapters 11 and 12 Paul the Apostle makes a defense of his apostleship based on his ability to endure hardship. Hey says apostles are given a death sentence (1 Cor. 4:9); because of the enormous responsibility they have to represent Christ, they are continually targets of persecution and criticism.

We also read in 2 Corinthians 12:5-11 that Paul was transparent and actually bragged about his weaknesses so the power of Christ could rest upon him. (This is unlike the preachers today who only brag about their faith and their accomplishments.)

*"On my own behalf I will not boast, except in regard to my weaknesses. For if I do wish to boast I will not be foolish, for I will be speaking the truth; but I refrain from this, so that no one will credit me with more than he sees in me or hears from me. Because of the*

*surpassing greatness of the revelations, for this reason, to keep me from exalting myself, there was given me a thorn in the flesh, a messenger of Satan to torment me—to keep me from exalting myself. Concerning this I implored the Lord three times that it might leave me. And He has said to me, 'My grace is sufficient for you, for power is perfected in weakness.' Most gladly, therefore, I will rather boast about my weaknesses, so that the power of Christ may dwell in me.*

*Therefore I am well content with weaknesses, with insults, with distresses, with persecutions, with difficulties, for Christ's sake; for when I am weak, then I am strong. I have become foolish; you yourselves compelled me. Actually I should have been commended by you, for in no respect was I inferior to the most eminent apostles, even though I am a nobody." -2* Corinthians 12:5-11

Apostolic truth includes the ability to function intelligently and spiritually in the midst of a high-stress environment.

Second Corinthians 11:23-33 says: *"Are they servants of Christ?—I speak as if insane—I more so; in far more labors, in far more imprisonments, beaten times without number, often in danger of death.*

*Five times I received from the Jews thirty-nine lashes. Three times I was beaten with rods, once I was stoned, three times I was shipwrecked, a night and a day I have spent in the deep. I have been on frequent journeys, in dangers from rivers, dangers from robbers, dangers from my countrymen, dangers from the Gentiles, dangers in the city, dangers in the wilderness, dangers on the sea, dangers among false brethren; I have been in labor and hardship, through many sleepless nights, in hunger and thirst, often without food, in cold and exposure. Apart from such external things, there is the daily pressure on me of concern for all the churches.*

*Who is weak without my being weak? Who is led into sin without my intense concern? If I have to boast, I will boast of what pertains to my weakness.*

*The God and Father of the Lord Jesus, He who is blessed forever, knows that I am not lying. In Damascus the ethnarch under Aretas the king was guarding the city of the Damascenes in order to seize me, and I was let down in a basket through a window in the wall, and so escaped his hands."*

Also in Acts 27 we see that Paul the Apostle remained calm and gave spiritual guidance to his captors while on the ship that crash-landed in Malta, resulting in a revival in Malta.

Apostolic ability is not based on comfort or circumstances but thrives in any environment, as we see Paul's worship in the Philippian jail which causes an earthquake and releases the prisoners (Acts 16).

## 2. Apostolic truth involves a deep understanding of the Scriptures and biblical truth

In the early church we find that the people sat under the apostle's doctrine (Acts 2:42). The apostolic mandate includes having a deep understanding of the Scriptures and essential biblical truth as well as church history, resulting in an ability to discern and correct biblical error before it leads to apostasy. (For example, the book of Galatians and book of Hebrews were written by an apostle to correct heresy.)

Apostolic doctrine is a balance between grace, holiness and truth, exalts the Lord Jesus above all, and the belief that the kingdom of God is advanced primarily through the local church.

Unfortunately, there are numerous reports of so-called apostolic leaders and/or movements that have embraced various extreme doctrines, which is due to leaders not being properly grounded biblically and historically. (Presently there is an extreme hyper-grace movement; an unbalanced prosperity gospel; extreme kingdom theology; and also liberation theology movements, to name only a few.)

**3. Apostolic truth cannot be separated from a deep and abiding relationship with Jesus**

The original Twelve Apostles all walked personally with Jesus, and the Apostle Paul encountered Jesus personally while on the road to Damascus (Acts 9). Paul also seemed to indicate that seeing Jesus was one of the things necessary to prove his apostleship (1 Corinthians 9:1-2):

*"Am I not free? Am I not an apostle? Have I not seen Jesus our Lord? Are you not my work in the Lord? If to others I am not an apostle, at least I am to you; for you are the seal of my apostleship in the Lord."*

Due to the enormous weight of responsibility for the churches and regions assigned to him, an apostle needs to be a person of prayer and continually aware of the presence and person of Christ to sustain him and enable him to walk in love and wisdom through numerous challenges they will face. If not, they will quickly make bad decisions and act in the flesh due to the enormous pressure constantly upon their lives.

Furthermore, their identity needs to be firmly rooted in Christ and not in their vast accomplishments or else they will minister out of a need to impress others and not for the glory of Christ.

They walk with Christ and worship Him even in the midst of great persecution and pressure. Apostolic ability is not based on comfort or circumstances but thrives in any environment.

## 4. Apostolic truth involves being strategic in planning and purpose

In 2 Corinthians 10:3-5 Paul says: *"For though we walk in the flesh, we do not war according to the flesh, for the weapons of our warfare are not of the flesh, but divinely powerful for the destruction of fortresses. We are destroying speculations and every lofty thing raised up against the knowledge of God, and we are taking every thought captive to the obedience of Christ."*

The word for war in verse three is the word strategy: Thus, Paul is saying that he is a divine strategist who, as a general in the Body of Christ,

leads the armies of God to conquer enemy territory

and present it back to the Lord Jesus.

One of the main characteristics I have observed in

true apostolic leadership is the acute ability to solve

problems, to take complex issues and simplify them,

and then to be able to map out a plan for strategic

implementation. It is not enough to have a vision; you

need to have the ability to strategically implement

the vision or it will be merely a dream.

**5. Apostolic truth includes reformation, not just revival**

The apostolic mandate is not about escaping the

earth but engaging culture with a goal of equipping

the saints to care for cities and nations. Thus,

apostolic theology teaches that an overseer of a key

church should shepherd their community, not just

their flock.

The apostolic not only deals with redeeming

individual sinners but also influences the systems

and social structures of communities, cities and nations. While revival brings people into the church, reformation has to do with sending the people out of the church into the world to reflect God's kingdom on earth as it is in heaven. Thus, apostolic truth exists to fulfill the Cultural Mandate of Genesis 1:28 and equip the saints to go into every sphere of society for kingdom influence and purpose.

In Ephesians 4:10-12 we also see the purpose of fivefold ministry is to equip the saints for the work of the ministry, which is to fill up the earth realm with kingdom influence under the Lordship of Christ.

## 6. Apostolic truth involves galvanizing unity in the church for a purpose

Apostolic truth is not merely ecumenical; that is to say, it does not strive merely for pastoral unity for the sake of unity, but it is based on a cause and purpose. Apostolic leaders will not waste time having unity that does not result in fulfilling kingdom purpose and destiny. They are not interested in pastors holding hands and fellowshipping with every so-called Christian and denomination and/or interfaith gatherings that do not result in expanding the influence of the kingdom in society. They will unite with likeminded churches and leaders to fulfill a certain mission in their cities and nations.

The Apostle Paul started churches in at least 30 of the most influential cities in the Roman Empire. Each of those churches started other churches until there was developed a complex apostolic network that was the impetus for world evangelization.

**7. Apostolic truth involves faith for finances and supernatural favor for doors to open**

Paul the Apostle constantly believed God for finances to support the work of God and even devoted two chapters to fundraising in 2 Cor. 8 and 9. He said that God would provide all of the Philippian church's needs in Philippians 4:19 because they supported his apostolic calling.

Apostolic truth is a mandate to believe for supernatural favor and finances to open doors and accomplish the ministry God called you to do. Thus apostolic leaders are always experiencing God's providence regarding guidance, favor and strategic opportunity for ministry (1 Cor. 16:9). Even more important than having money is having God's favor.

**8. Apostolic truth always builds and works through the local church first**

The apostolic mandate is connected inextricably to the local church, which is called by Paul the ground and pillar of the truth (1 Timothy 3:15). The gates of hell will not prevail against the church (Matthew 16:18) but can indeed prevail against any other institution not established by the church. Thus the apostolic leader doesn't want to waste time building on improper foundations that will not last.

The apostolic leader realizes that the gospels were written after the epistles, thus showing that Jesus always had the church in mind when He poured into the Twelve. This is important because many take the gospels as their model for discipleship in which they mentor individuals apart from connecting them to the corporate life and destiny of the local church, not understanding that Jesus had the church in mind when He was training the Twelve.

## 9. Apostolic truth involves the replication of apostolic leaders and organizations

Genesis 1 teaches us that every living thing reproduces life after its own kind. This is also true in the spiritual realm. The apostolic will always produce other apostles and apostolic churches, organizations and networks. The Bible is replete with examples of the power of reproduction and impartation. We see the influence of Jesus on the 11 apostles who changed the world, Paul's influence on Timothy, King David and his mighty men, Elijah and Elisha, Moses and Joshua, Samuel and the School of the Prophets.

The apostolic will be proven not only by the emergence of ministry but of apostolic ministry.

(Drawing a large crowd is not necessarily apostolic but can be evangelistic; harnessing the crowd to be societal transformers is what makes it apostolic.)

**10. Apostolic truth produces blueprints and a proper foundation based on enduring principles**

In 1 Corinthians 3 Paul calls himself a wise master builder (architect), which indicates that apostolic truth includes designing a blueprint that will lay a proper foundation for individuals and organizations.

Many make the mistake of going off into strange doctrines or getting distracted with numerous projects and programs while missing the simplicity of the gospel of Christ (2 Cor. 11:1-3).

Apostolic truth is one that works through the local church and focuses on winning the lost, equipping them, and sending them out to transform the world; apostolic leaders are not interested in any doctrine or program that does not point to this foundational work. Not only that, but they are able to design a plan for a network of churches that uniquely fits the contexts of their cultures, cities and nations. The principles they build upon are universal biblical principles that pastors, evangelists, and teachers can build upon which enable the saints to flourish.

**11. Apostolic truth includes a strong prophetic discernment of the will of God**

The Apostle Peter was the first person to receive a spiritual revelation of the identity of Jesus (Matthew 16). Paul's apostolic ministry was not given to him by men but by a revelation of Jesus Christ (Galatians 1). Paul was led to Western Europe instead of Asia due to a vision he had while sleeping (Acts 16). He regularly had visions that instructed him on what to do in challenging situations (Acts 18:9; 27:23). Even his apostolic mandate had strong prophetic implications (Acts 22:14-15).

It is my experience that apostolic truth includes strategy that emanates directly from the Spirit of God and not from mere intellect.

True apostolic leaders need to be continually led by the Spirit and not by mere emotion, circumstances or other people's opinions. Thus apostolic theology depends greatly on the prophetic to work.

## 12. Apostolic truth is one that has convening influence to determine the direction of the church

In Acts 15 we see the first general council of the church in which all the apostolic leaders from the entire world convened to decide the doctrine regarding non-Jewish believers in Messiah.

Apostolic truth is not just a concept but also a true influence over a region and/or a movement of churches. In this instance we see Peter, James and John convening a meeting with Paul and other key apostles.

It is my experience that apostolic truth must include convening power in particular spheres of influence as we read in 2 Corinthians 10:10-14. Each community should have at least one leading apostle who has convening power to direct the movement of the Body of Christ. In large cities such as New York, which has numerous networks, denominations and ethnic groups, there will likely be several key apostolic leaders with convening influence.

Also, this general council shows how all the apostles were accountable; they could not teach or preach anything they wanted. The one with the most convening authority was James, the half-brother of the Lord Jesus, who seemed to have the final say over everyone else.

# CHAPTER 10

# DOMESTICATING LIONS: THE TRAGIC ELIMINATION OF THE APOSTOLIC FROM THE CHURCH

It is tragic when the vast potential of an individual or entity is limited or eliminated because there is no room for their gifts. In the case of a lion, when captured and encaged it loses its aggressive roar because it is forced to be localized into the confines of a cage. It may be a lion but it is no different from a house cat because, like a house cat, it no longer has to claim its territory and hunt to satisfy its hunger, and is content to stay confined within a building.

To me, all of this is related to the condition of the local church after it ceases to recognize the ministry and function of apostolic leadership. This results in cutting off the pioneering spirit and apostolic call to conquer and expand kingdom influence.

(I don't necessarily think people have to use the title of apostle; the function is what is most important.)

In the case of church history, centuries ago we replaced the title (and consequently the function) of apostle and replaced it with the office of bishop. This vastly changed the nature and mission of the local and universal church. Apostles in the New Testament were the "sent ones" who, as military generals, were called to lead the church in mission as they were sent out to conquer new territories by planting churches and kingdom influence in key cities of the old Greco-Roman world. (For example, Paul the Apostle started churches in over 30 key cities before the commencement of the first century!) The office of bishop was primarily meant to oversee and administrate local churches: first starting in a local church (1 Timothy 3) which then evolved into overseeing a parish, then a diocese and then a region that included other bishops (hence they became archbishops or metropolitan bishops). However, as bishops became the apostolic successors it connoted a change from adventure, pioneering and conquering new territories (e.g. Paul, who prioritized going where Christ was not named as we read in 2 Corinthians 10:10-14) to one of settling and maintaining the church and focusing primarily on church life, polity and politics.

Not only that, but after the Protestant Reformation many (in response to the abuse of the bishops and popes) even eradicated the office of bishop and opted instead for a Presbyterian form of government (whether for good or bad) which only recognizes pastors, elder and teachers in the church. The eradication of the bishopric further isolated and fragmented the emerging evangelical church and resulted in numerous denominations and independent local churches. (For example, when the Eastern Church split from Roman Catholicism in the 11th century it remained virtually unified and intact because they kept the bishopric and/or the episcopate.)

Getting back to apostolic ministry, it is essential that we recapture the function (if not the title) of apostolic ministry once again so the lions of the church are released from their cages to go out and hunt (metaphorically speaking) and expand kingdom influence! The early church never saw their congregations as separate from the apostolic ministry and function of their recognized apostles. As a matter of fact, for them local church and mission were inextricably connected to the apostolic, not only in word but in finances! Read 2 Corinthians chapters 8 and 9, as well as Philippians 4 to see how local churches founded by Paul the Apostle supported his apostolic calling and ministry (and not just their local congregations) and even sent people from their congregations to accompany him on his trips (e.g. Epaphroditus in Philippians 2, Barnabas in Acts 13, Silas in Acts 15). Furthermore, Paul would install (pastoral) elders to care for the local congregations (Titus 1) and those who developed in the apostolic would travel with Paul to win new territory and/or establish the churches that were already founded. (For example, the epistles and the book of Acts highlight Timothy and Titus as well as some others who functioned apostolically with Paul to oversee churches and perform apostolic mission.)

Consequently, with the eradication of the apostolic from the local church, pastors have become the leaders of congregations. This has resulted in the body of Christ being led by caregivers instead of by strategic (military) generals sent out to conquer and establish new territory for the kingdom! The result has been disastrous as most churches have now become self-focused and inbred instead of kingdom-focused and mission centered.

The first church was born on Pentecost Sunday with an apostolic/prophetic message by the Apostle Peter. As we read the book of Acts, as long as the church was led by apostles it was constantly expanding and turning culture and cities upside down (Acts 17:6). The church was born in apostolic mission and it was meant to continue to be connected to its original mission of preaching the gospel to all creation and discipling nations (Mark 16:15-18 and Matthew 28:19)! As we have seen in the last fifty years in evangelicalism the focus has now become "church growth" and the apostolic message of the New Testament has now become watered down to accommodate culture instead of transforming it—of encouraging Christians merely to witness instead of winning others. The result is we have "mere" Christians who come to be entertained by professional worship teams instead of disciples who bring Christ in their marketplace mission field. True disciples should minister Monday to Saturday and not depend on inviting their friends to Sunday services to hear their pastor (a professional cleric) preach a salvation message in order for their unsaved friends to get saved!

Contrary to this, in the book of Acts and the gospels the majority of all ministry, including salvations and healings, took place outside the temple and synagogue. They even had extravagant moves of the Holy Spirit in the streets without the hype and correct atmosphere we typically need to see God do a miracle during a Sunday service! (Acts 5 shows that even the shadow of the Apostle Peter healed the sick in the streets and Acts 8 shows how Philip turned a whole city upside-down with miracles in the street.)

As the church becomes more and more inbred and self-focused (because the apostolic has been rejected) many Sunday messages have to do with "self-actualization" and "self-empowerment" or motivational messages that build crowds who couldn't give a hoot about the deteriorating political, social, economic and moral landscape of their communities. As we are lifting up our hands and praising God on Sundays 3,000 babies are being aborted per day and issues of poverty, injustice and alternate forms of family are being propagated by secular humanists who have captivated the minds of the millennials.

Furthermore, when apostles lead local churches an apostolic spirit of wisdom, revelation and courage comes upon entire congregations and releases all the saints to the work of the ministry (Ephesians 4:12) to fill up all things in creation (Ephesians 4:10). This produces (marketplace) apostles and prophets of government, economics, education, science, media and creative innovators that are at the (prophetic) tip of the spear by applying the biblical worldview to their spheres of influence. Hence, when a local church and/or movement of churches is not apostolically led and prophetically influenced they lose ground in their communities and culture because the apostolic mission of the church has been stripped away. Then, they become settlers who shy away from exercising bold faith and taking risks, and are more concerned about maintaining what they have.

While I am not against feeding the flock on Sunday and having great pastors who establish churches with great programs for their congregations, I am very concerned that we have a great lack of balance because of a lack of apostolic input. Furthermore, things have become twisted because of the American consumerist "I, me, my" culture; even some bona fide apostolic leaders with influential local congregations have become more concerned with building their own empires than for the things of the kingdom. In conclusion I believe the following:

- Local churches need to embrace and celebrate the ministry and function of apostolic leaders so their congregations can be connected to an ever expanding horizon of ministry that is called to influence every realm of life and plant centers of influence in every major city of the world (a la Paul the Apostle).

- We need to embody the apostolic spirit in our local churches so that all the members called to the secular arena will carry with them apostolic revelation and courage so they are not merely witnessing but transforming their workplaces and culture.

- Local church pastors need the input and inspiration of apostolic leaders to be balanced in regards to their church mission and vision.

- Local churches and movements need to nurture apostolic leaders and financially support them so each local church is connected to apostolic vision and mission that is beyond their community and religious subculture. Thus they will continue to be pioneers instead of settlers who are continually in maintenance mode.

Finally, unless the body of Christ once again celebrates the ministry function of apostle, some of the greatest leaders in our generation will never emerge (or will be repelled) because "like begets

like."

## CHAPTER 11

## TRUE DIFFERENCES BETWEEN APOSTOLIC AND

## PROPHETIC FUNCTION

There has been much confusion regarding the difference between apostolic and prophetic function.

Regarding these two functions, when we examine the Scriptures we find only a slight difference regarding ability in executive leadership roles, the main difference being the actual ministerial expression of leadership ability.

Many view prophetic ministers as folks who merely float from one place to the next as itinerant ministers who give "words of the Lord" to individuals and organizations, but have little or no ability to lead large, effective organizations. This definition is not sufficient in light of biblical teaching and models. Ministers who function like this may very well be "exhorters" who have a prophetic edge rather than functioning in the office of New Testament prophet.

When using the Old Testament as our guide, we find that many of the men called prophets were serving in roles that most today would consider apostolic. Men like the patriarch Abraham, Moses, and Samuel would certainly be called apostolic leaders if they were functioning in the same capacity in this day and age. Why they were called prophets and not apostles is the main subject of this brief essay.

Perhaps, one could say, the reason is because Old Testament prophets were the equivalent of New Testament apostles with no real difference in function or calling. Furthermore, when we read Ephesians 2:20 which says the church has been built upon the foundation of the apostles and prophets, we could say the word "prophets" in this passage is not referring to New Testament apostle/prophet teams but only to Old Testament prophets since the New

Covenant was based upon the prophetic writings that were handed down (a position I agree with).

That being said, if we find no real separation between apostles and prophets, then why separate apostolic and prophetic ministerial functions as we see in 1 Corinthians 12:28 and Ephesians 4:11?

As we examine the Scriptures, perhaps the real reason for this New Testament separation does not lie in the governmental nature and ability of New Testament prophets but lies in the fact that, in the Old Testament, prophets were mainly called to minister in a single geographic location because God was building a theocratic model-nation in Israel. (with the exception of the excilic and postexcilic prophets)

Even Acts 13:1-2 teaches that the great first-century church in Antioch was led by prophets. There was no mention of apostles in that church. This shatters the false assumption that present-day prophetic leaders cannot lead huge organizations or networks.

Since the resurrection of Christ and His command to take the gospel to every nation, we now have powerful leaders with anointings to go into uncharted enemy territories (where Christ has not been named or where there is no real kingdom witness), outside of the bounds of their local congregations, to set up beachhead ekklesias as salt and light to establish God's dominion in every territory.

This view goes along with the nature of the title "apostle" which literally means "a sent one." This term was taken from the Roman army, which called generals whom they sent to set up beachheads in enemy territory "apostles."

So, even though prophets were sent (Isaiah 6:6-9) they were mainly stationary in regards to their national focus. Apostles were deployed as God's generals to establish His kingdom witness in new nations and arenas of life.

If my above opining is true, then many people whom we today call apostolic are really New Testament prophetic leaders, and many of those we call prophets are merely exhorters who have a mature gift of prophecy (1 Corinthians 14:3 teaches on the nature of this gift of prophecy), and there are really far less apostolic leaders among the ranks of those who give themselves the title "apostle"!

To expound a bit more: What seems to be the main difference between apostolic and prophetic leaders in regards to their actual ministry mode and delivery? From experience it seems that when apostolic leaders engage in problem solving, teaching, or strategizing they tend to speak more out of principle--out of the accumulation of their vast experience. In contrast, prophetic leaders engaging in the same kind of problem solving have a different mode of delivery based on a more spontaneous, prophetic utterance. The difference is minute.

The point is, both can be involved in laying the foundation and the building of a local church or network of churches and establishing organizations. This is why they should both work in tandem to establish a kingdom witness on the earth.

While prophets may tend to speak into an entity that is already established, and apostles tend to be the initial leaders in establishing entities, both are needed and necessary--the apostle for breaking and establishing new ground, biblical purpose, and order in enemy territory, and prophets for bringing fire, passion, and a continual sense of urgency into the faith communities of those entities established by apostles.

In saying this, I realize it would be a huge mistake to imply that apostolic leaders are not prophetic. On the contrary, apostolic leaders must be extremely prophetic because, when being sent to lay a foundation and establish a beachhead for God in enemy territory, they must receive a word from God in regards to the timing, the geographic location, and the strategic spiritual warfare needed in order to be successful in their missions. Those functioning apostolically must have an acute sense of the leading of the Lord at all times. Hence, apostolic leaders have profound prophetic ability. It is simply that the primary focus of their ministries is on the managing, developing, and administration of leadership and the establishment of church government, whereas prophetic leaders have as their primary focus the renewal and continued movement towards hitting the mark in regards to corporate purpose and power.

In conclusion: Based on the realities presented above, perhaps there are really more apostolic and prophetic leaders working together than we think. Moreover, maybe it is not just those we deem apostolic leaders, but also true prophetic leaders who tend to shy away from some of the more extravagant, showy, shallow, itinerant prophetic ministers out there today. This is because true New Testament prophets are so principle-centered they cannot relate to those who exhort, make prophetic proclamations, and then leave with little or no accountability or oversight. True New Testament prophetic leaders are builders, not just blessers and, as such, maybe there is not really such a great present-day divide between apostolic and prophetic leaders.

Finally, I have seen many apostolic leaders working very closely with prophetic leaders in ways they cannot avoid: many apostolic leaders are married to prophetic spouses.

# CHAPTER 12

## THE DANGERS OF PURSUING YOUR CALLING WITHOUT THREE LEVELS OF COVERING

During the past several decades I have seen or read about more and more executive-level leaders and pastors falling into scandal or leaving the ministry because of personal challenges. Sometimes it seems like I hear about a leadership fall every week.

### The Need for Personal Alignment and Accountability

One thing many of these leaders have in common is their lack of (functional) personal alignment for their personal lives and/or ministries. By "personal alignment" I am referring to having either an individual spiritual mentor and/or guide who serves as your overseer who also has the authority to remove you or advocate for you in a time of moral failure or crisis. (I don't usually use the term "covering" but rather "overseer" because that is the more biblical term. But for the sake of relating better to my audience I am using the term "alignment" in this particular article.)

Many leaders (including myself) have one primary person who serves as their overseer but who is also part of a group of leaders that serve as their presbytery, these hold the leader accountable and can serve as mediators in case their standing as senior leader is in question, or if there is a need for mediation between them and their board of directors and leadership team.

A personal overseer has to be relational. This means it will only work if the senior leader is in regular dialogue with their overseer, and is honest regarding their personal challenges. One major minister who fell into scandal last year actually had a lot of close relationships and even prayed every morning with a close friend of mine. But, the problem was he never fully opened up regarding his dark side and sexual proclivities. Hence, having a close personal relationship with your overseer is never enough if you are not open and transparent with them. This is why I am using the modifier "functional" with "personal oversight and alignment."

When a senior leader doesn't have an honest, open, transparent relationship with a person who serves as their primary overseer, it can be a disaster waiting to happen! All leaders go through challenging times and need a person who can correct, encourage, rebuke or exhort them to continue to pursue God's calling in their life. Even if a leader never falls into sin, they may be accused of a sinful act and their church or organization may need to have an outside overseer or presbytery they can rely upon to investigate and/or mediate between both parties, to help them sort out what is true from what is false, and what strategic steps they should take for the good of the organization. Woe to the leader who has no one to confide in, turn to for advice, remove him/her or advocate for them in a time of crisis! In this context, you can almost view an overseer as fire insurance: you never know if and when you will ever need it, but if a serious situation arises that can threaten your place as the senior leader of an organization you will be thankful you had the prescience to purchase it.

Senior pastors' pressing need for alignment is one of the primary reasons I started Christ Covenant Coalition in 1999 (www.christcovenantcoalition.org). We are able to provide personal presbyteries for senior pastors in crisis as well as provide invaluable vertical and horizontal mentoring and coaching.

## The Need for Organizational Alignment

Related to this, I believe every senior leader needs to have organizational oversight, which is usually provided by the elders or trustees of an organization. Whenever any major decision is made related to vision and/or finances, every senior leader should first process it through with these highly trusted leaders. I know many leaders who failed to do this and made major strategic or financial mistakes that in some cases cost them their ministries, all because they didn't enable their board of directors to be an intricate part of major decisions they were making. Several senior pastors I know went out on a limb in purchasing properties because "the Lord told them" and made these decisions on their own without consulting their elders or trustees.

Unfortunately, in most cases like this, the leader made a huge blunder and even risked losing their whole ministry by plunging their work into huge debt, because they didn't receive counsel from their trusted team of leaders. Even though I believe in one senior leader serving as the first among equals who can have the final say in important matters, I also believe in leading from consensus with your primary team as much as possible to protect the organization and the leader from making foolish mistakes that occur when functioning in isolation, not in cooperation, with your primary leaders.

(Also when it comes to purchasing a building in which the whole congregation will be called upon to finance the vision, I believe it would also be wise for a senior pastor to hold a congregational meeting and receive the blessing of the whole church before proceeding forward with a large-scale building program.)

## The Need for a Prayer Covering

Another kind of alignment that is essential for every senior leader is a prayer covering. I have a regular team of people in our local church who are committed to praying daily for myself, my wife and family. This has been essential the past two decades regarding our ability to persevere in the midst of life's challenges. Scripturally, we also find that one of the primary parts of the armor of God is having the saints persevering in prayer for one another, even as Paul the apostle solicited prayers from the saints for his ministry (Ephesians 6:18-20).

Recently, the Lord spoke to me about the need to ramp up my prayer support because of a new sphere of influence and ministry I am walking into. With every new level there comes with it a higher devil. Thus, we need to pray and have intercession commensurate with the call of God upon our lives. Even though I usually spend a lot of private time seeking God every morning, I know I need outside help, even those functioning at a very high level in intercession on a national scale, to protect me and my family, and enable me to press into every area of opportunity God opens up for me and my team.

For example, I remember reading 19th century evangelist Charles Finney's autobiography and being impressed that he had personal intercessors (Father Nash and Abel Clary) who would go ahead of him into every town and lock themselves up in a room for days at a time, interceding and groaning in the Spirit, birthing in travail for revival. This was done even though Finney himself would usually spend hours every day seeking God and interceding for his ministry. This little-known fact is one of the primary reasons why Finney became the greatest revivalist the United States (and perhaps the world) has ever seen.

In summary I posit that, in order for every senior leader to be effective, we need to have at least three levels of alignment: personal oversight, organizational oversight, and a prayer covering that goes beyond our own prayer lives. If a leader functions with this level of accountability then their chances of failing and/or falling will be greatly diminished.

# CHAPTER 13

## THE MINISTRY OF APOSTLE IN CONTEMPORARY TIMES

The book of Ephesians 4:10-16 teaches us that the ministry gift of apostle will continue to function so that Christ can fill all things (every realm of society) until we come to full maturity in Christ as a church. Obviously these two things have not yet happened. So the question arises: What would the ministry of apostle look like in today's world?

Without qualifying all my statements due to the brevity of this article, the following are some observations and opinions I have related to this ministry in context with today's world. There have been many wonderful books written on the subject of the fivefold ministry (my favorite is Kevin Conner's The Church in the New Testament). Thus, there is no need for me to repeat content found in these other fine books.

Those walking in the apostolic ministry have a strong leadership gift (Romans 12:7). They are not primarily followers who conform to the mainstream but are willing to go against culture and carve out a countercultural movement that is based on the reign of God on earth as it is in heaven (read Acts 4:19-31). Thus, they are willing to lead a strong movement even in spite of religious and political opposition.

Contemporary apostles need to be able to preach the gospel and lead countercultural movements that can effectively deal with postmodernism (that there are no absolute truths that can be known in this world) and a post-taboo world (a classical Greek-Libertarian approach in which we live and let live; people can engage in any behavior they want with legal protection, for example alternate forms of marriage, abortion, euthanasia). This they do in a manner that does not make Christians come off as ignorant, uneducated biblicists but in a cogent, compelling manner that utilizes logic, godly wisdom, current events, statistics, and artful subtlety with the power of the Word and Spirit of God.

Apostolic leaders have the ability to manage whole networks of people, congregations and ministries that are relevant to and thrive in the midst of cultural complexities because they can adapt their methods and message based on the culture in which they labor.

For example, Paul established complex apostolic networks in over 30 diverse cities in the Roman world. He had to speak messages and build churches relevant to Jews (Acts 9, 21, 28), intellects (Acts 17:16-34) and people steeped in carnality and debauchery (First and Second Corinthians). He was not just an evangelist who blessed people and then left town; he was a master builder (1 Corinthians 3:10-14) who had a long-term plan to build communities of faith in the main cities of the Roman world (Ephesus, Philippi, Corinth, Colossae, Rome, Thessalonica) so they would eventually alter the culture and turn the world upside down (Acts 17:6; 19:21-41).

In today's world God is still using global leaders in India, Africa, Latin America, the USA, Asia and other places to start non-denominational complex apostolic networks that are driving missions across the earth.

**Apostles develop new emerging leaders**

When Paul met Timothy he immediately perceived that he was someone worth investing in to develop as a leader (Acts 16:1-3). Scripture teaches us that Paul's intuition was correct; we read that Timothy turned out to be Paul's best protégé (Phil. 2:19-25). Perhaps the most important calling of apostles is to see and develop the leadership potential in others.

In today's contemporary, fatherless world apostolic leaders are going to have to learn how to be fathers who can re-parent and bring healing to the fatherless, so potential leaders will have the internal affirmation necessary to become great leaders.

## Apostles are humble and broken, not superstars in their own minds (2 Corinthians 12:1-7)

Scripture teaches us that Paul ministered out of his weakness, not his strength. In today's world, I am skeptical of the superstar celebrity leaders who are always bragging about their ministries and accomplishments. Today we need authentic, transparent apostolic leaders who minister out of their weakness, as Paul did, so the glory and power are from Christ alone and to Him alone!

## Apostles have seen Jesus

In Acts 1 we see the 11 apostles attempted to choose a person that had walked and talked with Jesus personally to take the place of Judas Iscariot who fell away from his calling and committed suicide. In 1 Corinthians 9:1 and Acts 22:14 an important part of Paul's calling to the apostolic was that he had seen Jesus personally. Whether this was in the body or just a vision we don't know (2 Corinthians 12). But the main idea is that Paul had a powerful life-changing encounter with Jesus that rooted and grounded him in the faith and gave him an intimacy with Christ that sustained him through all his trials and tribulations.

Contemporary apostles (like Moses and Paul of old) need to know the Lord face-to-face as a man knows his friend (Deut. 34:10) so they can clearly hear His voice and have faith to walk in great exploits, and so they are not walking in presumption and embarrass themselves and the gospel.

## Apostles move in signs, wonders and miracles (Romans 15:18-20; 2 Corinthians 12:12)

Paul and the other New Testament apostles regularly moved in miraculous signs, wonders and miracles which included gifts of healings, working of miracles and casting out demons.

In contemporary times this is not only related to the aforementioned supernatural signs, but the signs of God's providential favor—being at the right place at the right time, supernatural doors opening up, financial provisions miraculously coming for ministry projects, and great faith to see God do supernatural things in the hearts and minds of people so the great apostolic vision God has given them can be accomplished.

**Apostles speak in principle what prophets prophesy by revelation**

The apostolic leaders I know, like John Kelly speak in principle words of wisdom that constantly flow out of them, even in ordinary spontaneous conversations. This is unlike many prophetic people who depend upon the Spirit to come upon them and prophesy to give a word of wisdom. Both are effective; that's why prophets and apostles complement one another and give each other balance.

**Apostles are great problem solvers and strategists**

Apostolic leaders are able to look at a project and think of all contingency plans (and even have a plan

A, B, C based on what happens) like no other leaders. They can take the complex and make it simple for all to understand. They are master builders who can come into a disorganized church or ministry and bring great order within a short period of time. While others see reality in bits and pieces, apostolic leaders can put all the pieces of the puzzle together; they plan ahead, see life at light speed, and see all of life like a chess player who plans ten moves ahead.

**Apostles are great fundraisers and operate in the gift of faith for new territories**

Apostolic leaders, like Paul, are great visionaries who can motivate people and churches to give to the things of the kingdom (read 2 Corinthians 8, 9).

I have never met a true apostle who didn't have great vision as well as faith and strategy to believe and receive provision for the vision. This is one of the main ways to distinguish between true and false apostles. False apostles may have apostolic teaching and revelation, and call themselves apostles on their business cards. But they have never built anything of substance. True apostles not only talk but walk the walk with provision for the vision so they can build great works for the Kingdom of God. This is because they have learned to trust God to meet their needs as well as to touch the hearts of potential donors who can fund the vision.

**Apostles usually don't focus on minutia but see the big picture**

Apostolic leaders usually miss the tree because they see the forest. They usually do not have much patience for one-on-one counseling unless it is with a high-level leader they are mentoring. This is not because they do not have compassion but because God has wired them to focus on the big picture. Apostolic leaders are "high D" doers and are satisfied more in accomplishing tasks. If they had grace for minutia and hand-holding they would spend most of their time doing those things and would not have the emotional and spiritual energy left for the larger picture of the vision God has assigned to them. Thus, apostolic leaders have learned to nurture pastoral leaders who do the counseling, coaching and hand-holding that the congregation needs.

In closing, we need to greatly value the gift of apostle in our midst. God says this gift is so important that when He starts a work He first sets in an apostle to lay the foundation before any other office or function is established, thus ensuring that the whole building will have the proper foundation (read 1 Corinthians 12:28).

# CHAPTER 14

## THE OFFICE OF PROPHET AND CONTEMPORARY TIMES

There has been much written about the office and function of prophet in the past three decades. In this article I will be writing regarding my own experience in understanding what the Bible says about the prophetic ministry, and I will attempt to connect this to today's world.

First of all, by prophet I am not referring to a person who exercises the gift of prophecy as taught in 1 Corinthians 14:2-4 (consisting of general exhortations, comfort and rebuke, which everyone in the church is encouraged to do; read 1 Corinthians 14:39). I am also not referring to a person preaching a sermon to a congregation. I am speaking about a person who, through much prayer, travail, and meditation in the scriptures, regularly stands in the council and heavenly assembly of God (with the angels and other messengers of God's court) to hear what the Spirit is saying, so that the mind and heart of God can be communicated to the church and nation. Examples of a prophet standing in the council and/or court of the living God to hear His word are found in Isaiah 6:1-9; Ezekiel 1-3,10; Jeremiah 15:19; extraordinary examples of this can be found in the New Testament with the Apostle Paul in 2 Corinthians 12:1-12 and the Apostle John in Revelation 1:9-20 and 4:1-2.

Jeremiah 23:16-22 shows that the main distinction between false and true prophets is that false prophets speak without being in the council of the Lord and, hence, utter words without ever being sent by God.

David Chilton says the following about prophets in his book The Days of Vengeance: "The prophets not only observed the deliberations of the heavenly Council (cf. 1 Kings 22:19-22); they actually participated in them. Indeed, the Lord did nothing without consulting His prophets (Amos 3:7). This is why the characteristic activity of the Biblical prophet is intercession and mediation (cf. Gen. 18:16-33; 20:7, the first occurrence of the word prophet in Scripture). As members of the Council the prophets have freedom of speech with God, and are able to argue with Him, often persuading Him to change His mind (cf. Ex. 32:7-14; Amos 7:1-6). They are His friends, and so He speaks openly with them (Gen. 18:17; Ex. 33:11; 2 Chron. 20:7; Isa. 41:8; John 15:15). As images of fully redeemed Man, the prophets shared in God's glory, exercising dominion over the nations (cf. Jer. 1:10; 28:8), having been transfigured ethically (cf. Isa. 6:5-8) and physically (cf. Ex. 34:29). They thus resembled the angels of heaven, and so it is not surprising that the term angel (Heb. mal'ak, Greek angelos) is used to describe the Biblical prophet (cf. 2 Chron. 36:15-16; Hag. 1:13;

Mai. 3:1; Matt. 11:10; 24:31; Luke 7:24; 9:52)" (page 82).

**So how do those standing in the office of prophet function in today's world?**

**First of all**, prophets are people who regularly engage in deep intercession and travail for the purposes of God to be fulfilled on the earth. Whenever a person is in true Spirit-led travail of soul, they are literally standing in the council of God— participating and pleading with God to have His way on the earth. A person who has no such deep experience with God will probably only be able to move in the simple gift of prophecy (1 Corinthians 14:2-4) and not function in the office of prophet for the nation or church.

**Second of all**, true prophets take what they hear from God in the heavenly courts and pray or pronounce the will of God by faith, so that His will is done and His kingdom comes on earth as it is in heaven (Luke 11:2). When it is spoken in prayer, they are pronouncing divinely inspired orders from God that are then transmitted from the throne room to the angelic beings (both good and bad) who serve as the spiritual archetypes that influence the earth realm (read Matthew 18:18-19; Ephesians 3:10).

**Third**, prophets can also be preachers who don't only come with prepared sermons based on human wisdom of words but speak a specific word to the church and/or people that they heard from God in the heavenly courts. This kind of preaching transforms individuals and congregations because the force and authority of the Holy Spirit is behind it, and is manifest as a rhema word (Hebrews 4:11-13).

**Fourth**, prophets have a deep thirst to be in the presence of God and meditate on the word of God so they can actually engage God in the scriptures while God burns His searing hot truth and light into their being. This in turn enables the prophet to understand how to apply the word of God to the people or situation he or she is confronting, counseling or speaking into.

**Fifth**, prophets have an understanding of the times in which they live (1 Chron. 12:32). Through both natural knowledge (from reading newspapers, books, and interaction with high-level societal leaders) and spiritual knowledge (when in prayer or fellowship with God) they are able to take the natural knowledge they have assimilated and present it with clarity, divine accuracy and power! Thus prophets not only read the Bible but also keep up with current events so they can apply the word to contemporary situations.

**Sixth**, prophets always have a window open to God in their souls, resulting in them regularly moving in words of knowledge, words of wisdom, discerning of spirits and prophecy, even when they are not engaged or totally focused in an act of prayer or in a church service or setting. Thus they are always in fellowship with the person and presence of God and are able to hear what He is saying at a moment's notice, even in the midst of their mundane, daily activities.

My friend, Hubert Synn, serves as an extraordinary example of this. Once while he was walking in an airport terminal, he felt an impression to give a word of guidance to a total stranger, who was at that moment praying in his heart for divine guidance. The result of this prophetic word was confirmation for Pastor Jonathan Cahn to write the New York Times bestselling book The Harbinger.

I have often operated in this gift, but many times the person I am speaking to doesn't know it because my words come in the context of a regular conversation, yet with significant results. (I can give many examples of this but do not have space in this article.)

An examination in the gospels shows that Jesus regularly moved in words of knowledge as part of His evangelistic and prophetic ministry, to confirm His word to those He was speaking to (read John 4; Mark 2:8-10; 3:1-7).

**Seventh**, prophets do not have to be pastors or preachers, but can be marketplace leaders who function with a high degree of intimacy with God and use it in a profound way to engage culture and affect change in the lives of those they are working with. For example, read the prophet Daniel chapters 2, 4, 5 and the account of Joseph in Genesis chapters 40 and 41. These are two men who had secular jobs but utilized their prophetic callings to transform nations and empires.

Also, my prophetic friend mentioned in the previous point is not a full-time preacher but an accountant.

**Eighth**, prophets walk in the royal favor of God. Somehow they are usually at the right place and the right time. Thus, God is always providentially opening up doors for them or guiding them, even when they are not aware of it.

**Ninth**, prophets are able to divinely interpret the redemptive reasons for the suffering, pain, and seasons of life that people experience. They are able to give profound words of advice that can transform a life, answer a prayer, bring clarity to an enigma, or help a person discover their purpose, just with a short conversation, prayer or prophetic word. Whole books of the Bible like Isaiah, Jeremiah and Amos illustrate the power of prophets who are able to interpret the times and the seasons for the people and nation they live among.

**Tenth**, prophets are called to represent God to a people or nation and bring a covenant lawsuit to them (Micah 3:8). The word witness was originally a legal term regarding a person that was an aide to a person bringing a lawsuit, even to the point of being part of the legal process that involved execution! Thus, prophets who stand in the heavenly council as witnesses of the Lord not only hear God's will regarding a people or nation but can actually be part of the process that brings judgment to that person or people group.

Biblical examples of this include Elijah in 1 Kings 17:1, when the prophet declared to King Ahab that Israel would have a drought until his word released rain; Peter in Acts 5, when he pronounced judgment upon Ananias and Sapphira for lying; Paul in Acts 13, when he blinded Elymas the sorcerer for obstructing the gospel; and John in Revelation 1:3, when he bore witness to the words of Christ that resulted in bringing judgment on false Israel and the pagan systems of the world that Israel was in cahoots with.

Finally, most importantly, prophets have learned that those who are friends with politicians and wealthy people are a dime a dozen. But those who are intimate with God are very few on the earth! The most important function for a true prophet is to be a friend of God who knows God and speaks to Him face-to-face as a man speaks to his friend (Deuteronomy 34:10; John 15:15).

# CHAPTER 15

## TEN ESSENTIAL PRINCIPLES OF THE JERUSALEM APOSTOLIC CHURCH MODEL

Introduction

There is a need for the body of Christ to go back to the way of Jesus and the apostles as shown in the first-century church. In order to do this we must begin with the first church born after the resurrection of Christ. The best way forward to discover some important principles from this apostolic church is to go through the first several chapters of the Book of Acts.

**The following are some of the salient Jerusalem apostolic church principles extracted from the Book of Acts:**

**1. They needed to be immersed in heaven's perspective before they could function effectively on the earth (Acts 1-2).**

After the resurrection of Christ, the disciples were still looking for a quick fix via a manifestation of a triumphant political kingdom centered in Jerusalem (Acts 1:4-8). Jesus had to refocus them by commanding them to gain heaven's perspective through the power of the Holy Spirit, which would only come by waiting on God until they were endued with power from on high (Luke 24:49). The church was born out of a 10 day prayer meeting (gaining God's power and perspective cannot be rushed). Hence; the prayer meeting came before they attempted their mission on the earth. It is a mistake to think the church can fulfill the mission of God merely by strategy or by first immersing themselves in their communities.

First we need to immerse ourselves in heaven before we can be effective on the earth. The Book of Acts could also be called the book of prayer (Acts 1-4; 10; 13; and 16 all speak about significant things that came forth out of a "seeking" attitude and commitment to regular prayer). For 10 days the

original disciples prayed in the upper room, perhaps

it took this long for their paradigm to change because

of the many things the Spirit had to work inside of

them. The Spirit had to remind them of all of Jesus'

words spoken to them during the gospel period. The

Spirit had to reinterpret all those words in light of the

cross and resurrection. The Spirit had to immerse

them in the power and presence of God to turn their

cowardice into courage and their fear to faith.

**2. They devoted themselves to the apostle's**

**doctrine, to fellowship, to breaking of bread and**

**the prayers.**

They had all things in common, received their food

with glad and generous hearts, breaking bread in

their houses and continually praising God and having

favor with unbelievers (2:42-47).

After the download from the Spirit, which took

place over the course of the 10 day prayer meeting,

not just on the day of Pentecost, the apostles were

now able to interpret the implications of the death and resurrection of Christ to the people. This apostolic doctrine was mentioned first because it framed everything else they did. Their fellowship, breaking of bread, and prayer all came out of the context of being indoctrinated by the apostolic teaching. Mere fellowship and/or prayer without the apostolic framework are not effective and result in purposeless social gatherings and ritualistic prayer without power.

The effect of this apostolic paradigm was so profound it even affected the mundane things they did in their lives and turned ordinary dinners into a remembrance of the Lord's broken body, accompanied with great joy and gladness with every family meal.

They also lived in a state of continual praise and had favor with all the people (by implication, those outside the church). This implies that even the world will recognize genuine Christianity if it is practiced house-to-house and has imbued even the ordinary practices and attitudes of believers.

## 3. They had regular times of daily corporate prayer (Acts 3:1).

In the Levitical system there were morning and evening sacrifices. In this Jewish mindset, offerings were a type of prayer offered to God. Hence, the early church was used to praying and offering sacrifices at regular set intervals of the day. In this particular passage we see that the apostles were heading to the temple "at the hour of prayer" which happened to be 3 p.m. Many scholars believe the Jews went to the temple to pray everyday at 6 a.m., noon and 3 p.m., and perhaps even 6 p.m. The point is, the original apostolic church did not just depend upon once per week meetings to connect with God, but there were daily times set aside to pray. Later on in church history this pattern of daily prayer was called the "daily office".

**4. The leaders were biblically trained in their local faith community (Acts 4:13).**

When the religious leaders called Peter and John uneducated but took note that they had been with Jesus, they were referring to Peter and John's lack of formal training in the rabbinic school that taught the Torah and the traditions of the elders. Being biblically trained in the church family became the norm as all the believers matured into their calling in the context of the local church, not through being shipped away to a seminary. This becomes a critical issue to us in contemporary times because of the present failure to follow this biblical model for training leadership.

Typical denominations attempt to train potential church leadership in a seminary, which is out of the context of the faith community, often resulting in a failure to produce effective church-based leaders. This is why in our local church we utilize church-based theological education (http://www.bild.org), and recommend young people get a secular degree in a regular college. This educational strategy prepares the folks in our church for both the secular and church world without removing them from the covering and care of the local congregation.

**5. The apostolic church renounced material individualism, not private property (4:32-35).**

This section shows us that another important component of being an apostolic church is the renunciation of individualism even when it comes to material goods. Some would use this chapter to teach that the early church espoused a form of communism (in which no one lays claim to their right to own private property for the good of the secular state), but there is no such teaching in this passage.

This passage actually shows the reverse. It shows that the apostolic church used their private property for the glory of God rather than for the glory of the state or for self-gratification.

**6. The apostolic church experienced the judgment of God as well as spiritual renewals (Acts 5:1-11).**

In this chapter a mighty prayer meeting (4:26-31), a great move of corporate unity, and mutual care for each member's material needs were followed by the divine removal of one of the wealthiest financial contributors in the church. The removal of Ananias and Sapphira, not only from the church but from the earth, shows that a believer's life is not worth living if indeed it results in hurting the purity and mission of the church. This also illustrates the fact that God deems the unity and holiness of the church as more important than its material needs being met through high-end donors. (Often pastors will compromise the mission of the church to appease their highest tithers.) This chapter also shows us that sometimes when God shows up it is not for revival; it is for judgment.

**7. The apostolic church allowed God to move in the streets (5:12-16).**

It is no coincidence that the majority of the miracles in the gospels and Book of Acts were done in the streets, not in the synagogue or temple. The apostolic church is not a box church in which all the activities take place in a building on a Sunday morning. God wants to show off His stuff and prove the resurrection of His Son. The apostolic church brings Christ to the city and does not expect the city to come to the congregation without a demonstration of His power.

## 8. The apostolic church used every challenge as an opportunity (Acts 6:1-7).

When the Hebrews neglected the Greek speaking Jews in the daily distribution of food, the apostles refused to lose their focus on their primary calling, but used this challenge as an opportunity to empower more believers for the service of the church. This shows us there will always be challenges and problems in every local church, but apostolic churches turn every challenge into an opportunity to go to another level of effectiveness.

## 9. The apostolic church produced martyrs (Acts 7:59-60).

The blood of the martyrs became the seedbed of the early church. When Jesus told the church that the Holy Spirit would enable them to be witnesses, this is the Greek word martus from which we get the modern word martyr. Hence, being a witness for Christ was equated with dying for Christ.

Nowadays the church often produces self-centered believers who attempt to use their faith to live a life of ease and comfort rather than lay their whole life on the line for the master.

## 10. God forced the apostolic church to fulfill their mission to send out believers to fulfill His mission (Acts 8:8).

In spite of the commandment by Jesus to go into the entire world and preach the gospel (Mark 16:15), the Jerusalem church stayed in one community and one city and focused on just one ethnic people, the Jews. God had to allow a great persecution to break out to scatter the believers so that some of their best trained leaders could go and spread the gospel to other cities of the region. Sometimes God disrupts the normal pattern of life in a church to fulfill His greater purposes. Philip would have never turned the city of Samaria upside down if God did not send trouble and allow Stephen to be martyred.

# CHAPTER 16

## ESSENTIAL TRAITS OF THE APOSTOLIC CHURCH

The Antioch Church has been the model for missions movements, church planting, and urban reconciliation for almost 2,000 years. The following principles show why this church, rather than the Jerusalem Church, is the church model:

**I. The Antioch Church was an inclusive church that was born out of persecution (Acts 11:20)**

1. Often, people who are the victims of persecution and are experienced in the way of suffering are a more broad and broken people ready and willing to go out of their cultural box to welcome and love others, as opposed to the homogeneous model of the Jerusalem Church. Note that David said that God enlarged him when he was in distress; Psalm 4:1.

2. There is the real and the ideal; often those experienced in suffering have more compassion and

really know what it is like for God to love them unconditionally.

## II. The word over the Antioch Church was "purpose," which transcends earthly & material possessions, money, and concerns (Acts 11:23)

1. The apostolic church emphasizes God's kingdom purpose rather than material possessions, convenience, or comfort.

2. Often, people go by the voices of others or by their own feelings and circumstances. God has called His people to go by His purpose for their lives as their ultimate guide.

3. God's kingdom purpose is always corporate purpose; that is to say, our individual purpose will never be fulfilled unless it is attached to a local church.

## III. The Antioch Church had emerging fivefold ministry gifts (Acts 13:1)

1. They had prophets and teachers. No reference is made of apostles, pastors, or evangelists; thus I believe this was an emerging leadership.

2. Barnabas and Saul became apostles after they were sent out and continued to mature.

3. There was evidently some kind of discipleship process in which leaders were continually raised up. In Acts 11:26 the whole church was taught, implying that there was some personal process of mentoring. For example, cell groups or house meetings were common in those days, which would make sense because their leadership model was the Jerusalem Church which taught "house to house" (Acts 2:46).

## IV. The leadership and congregation were multiethnic (Acts 13:2)

1. The Jerusalem Church was multilingual and multiethnic but was not transcultural because they never reached out beyond Judaism.

2. The Antioch Church modeled ethnic reconciliation. There were five walls that divided the ethnic groups

in the city of Antioch; believers in this church would scale the walls to attend church together.

3. Believers today still need to be intentional and "scale the walls" that divide them from their ethnically or economically different brothers and sisters.

## V. The leadership was vocationally diverse (Acts 13:2)

1. Barnabas was into real estate; Saul was a religious leader; Manaen was a politician.

2. Scripture teaches that it takes more than a religious leader to transform a culture or nation (see the books of Esther, Nehemiah, Ezra, Daniel, etc.). We need to see an Antiochian leadership model that employs business, political, and religious leadership together to proclaim the kingdom of God.

## VI. They were a church that connected to God's presence

1. They regularly ministered to the Lord. Today's congregations only come to God to receive from the

Lord instead of ministering to the Lord. If we would learn to minister to the Lord then He would minister back to us beyond measure.

2. They heard from the Lord regarding mission and purpose. Many people just want to hear from the Lord regarding their own personal issues!

**VII. They were a sending church**

1. They understood and preached corporate mission and corporate destiny!

2. The members and leaders followed apostolic protocol in regards to their ministry. Nowadays most ministers "went" instead of being "sent." This is the reason why there are so many dysfunctional pastors and churches in this nation!

**VIII. They were a benevolent church and gave to other ministries and churches (Acts 11:29)**

1. A people who understand pain are also a people who empathize with the needs of others, which results in them being moved by compassion to give to others.

## Chapter 17

## Apostles and Apostolic Movements

Anyone observing what is taking place can't help but notice the proliferation of what has been termed "The Apostolic Reformation". A decade ago, our network of ministers, Christ Covenant Coalition, organized a conference dealing with this subject entitled "The Apostolic Revolution".

Understanding this move of God is so vital for the health and vibrancy of the church I felt the need just to summarize some of the key points needed to understand this term "Apostolic".

When I say "Apostolic", I generally use it as an adjective describing a function or a confluence of networks, associations of churches and ministries. It is not my primary intention to tag individuals with the title "Apostle".

Historically and in contemporary times, we have seen much abuse in regards to the presumptuous and even precocious use of this term, resulting in the further misunderstanding and alienation of many in the church when it comes to recognizing the Apostolic model today.

Furthermore, the term "Apostolic" when describing a movement also carries with it some unfortunate baggage within certain circles because some denominations with the title "Apostolic" have been autocratic in their leadership style while placing extra biblical (legalistic) demands on church members.

This is obviously not what I mean when I use the term "Apostolic".

Although I believe that all the ministry gifts mentioned in Ephesians 4: 11 continue to exist, and that there are many today that may have a legitimate claim to the ministry of Apostle, in this particular missive we are more concerned with understanding the function and flow of apostolic movements as a whole (perhaps we can describe this as a sort of new "wineskin" revolutionizing the church around the world).

**Some of the characteristics of Apostolic Movements are:**

I. Bible believing pastors and ministers voluntarily come together regionally to advance the Kingdom of God irrespective of their denominational affiliation and sectarian identities.

II. Ministerial leaders emerge who have an "apostolic anointing" to galvanize the Body of Christ in their region and give direction to the city church movement.

(This point scares some denominational leaders who exercise leadership over certain ministers and churches only because of political placement, organizational loyalty, seniority, and or administrative ability. Their gifting is more like that of an administrator than that of a pastor of pastors.

These folk more than most see the Apostolic

Movement as a threat because ministers under their

denominational authority may begin to gravitate

towards those in their region who have the

affirmation of the corporate body of Christ.

So, opposition against the Apostolic will most likely

be fueled more because certain religious leaders

believe it will undermine the influence they have in a

region–not because of theological disagreement).

III. The regional church begins to demonstrate their

unity publicly through various corporate events that

become visible expressions of the emerging "One City

One Church" reality in the Body of Christ. (They come

together for "Concerts of Prayer", "City Serve",

"Community Development Projects", "Ministerial

Associations", "Pastors Covenant and Accountability

Groups"...)

Pastors involved in these movements not only begin

to work together, they even begin to change their

language because of the change in the way they think

of the church in general:

A.  Examples of the language used:

1.  "One city, one church" -- In my region there is only

"One church, but many congregations".

2.  "A senior pastor is not primarily called to a local

church, but to shepherd a city"

IV. The united visible church begins to speak

prophetically to the culture and begins to influence

all of society, not just the church world.

A. Crime begins to drop.

B. Elected officials start to come to Apostolic and

Prophetic leadership for prayer, counsel and political

support.

C. More and more the spiritual climate of a

community begins to change as the Word-Law of God

once again becomes the standard and rule of law for

the community

V. Apostolic churches begin to emerge who:

A. Have a strong apostolic leader functioning as the senior pastor.

B. These churches employ a form of church government that involves a plurality of leaders under the leadership of an apostolic leader (Although this leadership or ministry team may have different names: Eldership team, Ministry team, Deacon board...they all flow out of the paradigm of a "multiplicity of ministries" instead of the "mom and pop shop" mode of church government. that is so common today in many local churches).

C. They continually raise up and send out ministers and ministries to plant churches, start new ministries that holistically affect whole communities, and place godly leadership in every sphere of society for the purpose of fulfilling the Great Commission in Matthew 28:19 that instructs the church to "Go and teach (disciple) all nations".

VI. Apostolic churches nurture and "mother" other pastors, ministers, and churches. Their concern is primarily with building the Kingdom of God and not their own empires.

They have learned to work and bless the Body of Christ in their locale and as such know they are called of God to serve the Kingdom, not just their local flock.

Consequently, as a nurturing church the whole community comes up to another level and the whole Body experiences church growth.

(This is in stark contrast to some of the mega churches that grow primarily off of the smaller "feeder churches" who lose many of their new converts to a church with more programs to offer). Instead of seeing how they can share their resources, minister to the pastors of smaller churches and help equip them to be more effective in their region, some mega churches actually focus the marketing of their ministry to the attendees of smaller churches.

(Though their church may experience tremendous growth, the Kingdom is not enlarged; they are merely "swapping fish". After awhile the fish begin to stink.)

There is much more that can be said. These were all generalizations and not meant to stereotype any particular individual or group. Within all of these descriptions are also vast variations within the groups and movements and so we are forced to merely classify and categorize but not reflect every possible situation within a movement or church. (For example, some Apostolic Movements are very loose with very little organization and financial commitments; others are well organized, require tithes or fees, credential their members, provide oversight and may even gather around some body of theological agreement).

This was not meant to be a polemic that engenders a judgmental attitude towards certain churches or denominations, but meant to provide a greater understanding of perhaps the most important reformation we have seen since the Protestant

Reformation in 1517.

# CHAPTER 18

## CONTRASTING APOSTOLIC MOVEMENTS FROM INSTITUTIONS AND DENOMINATIONS

The following are generalizations that may or may not be true for particular denominations and apostolic movements:

### I. Apostolic Movements vs. Denominations

1. Apostolic is usually led by one strong visionary/Denomination by a board.

2. Apostolic is usually mission driven/Denomination policy driven.

3. Apostolic is usually missiological in its biblical hermeneutic/Denomination is usually theological, sociological or culturally driven.

4. Apostolic emphasizes covenantal relationships based on voluntary associations/Denominations emphasize hierarchical structures and business in their gatherings.

5. Apostolic emphasizes the present move of God in the earth/Denominations the glory days of the past.

6. Apostolic emphasizes the movement/ Denominations the institution.

7. Apostolic leaders are led by the Spirit in regards to ministry placement/Denominational clergy are led by their bishop or hierarchy.

8. Apostolic believes in biblical inerrancy/Most denominations believe in a higher critical form of inspiration. (Their line of reasoning goes like this: because the church gave the Scriptures the church has the right to change them, update them, etc. through church councils and official writings. Another thing said is that only the actual words of Jesus Christ in the Gospels are inspired of God.)

9. Apostolic emphasizes the power of Christ in terms of releasing faith to fulfill ministry/Denominations the power of committees to implement strategic plans.

10. Apostolic emphasizes the local church as the primary training ground for ministry/Denominations emphasizes the seminary.

11. Apostolic empowers the laity to minister (Ephesians 4:11, 12)/In denominations the clergy are expected to do the work of the ministry.

**II. Strength of Denominations**

1. Have a connection to the historic creeds, confessions and church history.

2. Have infiltrated and have credibility in institutional systems.

3. Have a system of ordination, placement of ministry and criteria for ministry (seminary training, etc.).

4. Once started as movements and have cycled into institutions, thus they are ahead of the apostolic in the usual cyclical norm.

5. Have an understanding of culture and academia along with their theology (doesn't have an anti-intellectual bias in its churches).

6. Are involved in lobbying public policy issues (until recently the Catholic church had great political influence in the U.S. because of all of the above).

7. They generally have a clearly defined system of accountability.

### III. I Propose a New Synthesis of I and II

1. The Need for a Connection to Church History (John 17:21 in regards to the need for church unity has to be expanded to include the body of saints already in heaven, Hebrews 12:1.)

The apostolic leadership and churches needs to rejuvenate a love for the historic church writings including the creeds, confessions and theological writings of the church fathers. We need to believe according to Ephesians 4:11-16 that God has been building and the Holy Spirit has been teaching His church for the past 2,000 years. Ignorance of these writings is to dismiss God's historic activity in His church and hinders our ability to build upon the shoulders of those who have gone before us.

2. The Apostolic Should Synthesize Movement and Institution

We need to have both a movement and an institution so that our movement can institutionalize the ground we gain in the culture. Remaining merely a movement will marginalize us by keeping us on the fringe of society instead of infiltrating and reforming it.

3. The Need for Protocol in Regards to Apostolic Recognition

Key apostolic leaders need to convene an assembly whereby they come up with a consensus of protocol that can be used to propose how clergy can be set in and recognized as apostolic leaders and bishops. Too often these folks are self-appointed because there is no universally established protocol. This assembly can only make a proposal, but if key leaders make a unified statement (e.g. the Lausanne Covenant) it will pressure other leaders to follow its recommendations.

I believe at least the minimum procedure should be that seasoned, recognized apostolic leaders in a region should endorse and be a part of the process of setting in a person as a bishop or apostle.

4. The Need to Capitalize on the Cyclical Norms

Since all denominations once started off as an apostolic movement usually driven by a powerful visionary leader, those in the apostolic should learn how to allow for the cycle of movement to maintenance to institutionalization without compromising the missiological nature that gave it birth to begin with.

This can be done by:

- Laboring for continual revival and renewal.

-Keeping a steady flow of prayer, fasting and worship (the 17th century Moravians had a 100 year prayer meeting).

-Allowing for God to continue to burden us and activate us for missions and reformation.

-Discipling our spiritual and biological children, and exposing them to the cutting edge of what God is doing on the earth in their generation.

-Having a strategic plan of placing the right homegrown leaders in place to succeed the successful visionary leaders (too often the movement dies or goes into maintenance mode because the next leader is merely a good consolidator/administrator who lacks the passion of the original leader).

5. Apostolic Leaders should be Disciplined Learners and Have an Understanding of the Biblical Worldview, Theology and Apologetics

Apostolic leaders should return to studying both systematic and biblical theology and apologetics so they can train upcoming leaders with a biblical worldview capable of advancing them through the highest universities in academia (instead of being anti-intellectual and running from academia we should be infiltrating them and returning them to their original purpose). Most apostolic leaders are

Biblicists who are not well read or well rounded and thus unable to prepare, equip and relate to those who will lead in various realms of society.

6. Apostolic Leaders are now Called to Apply the Biblical Worldview to Public Policy as a Method of Propagating the Kingdom

The next advance for the apostolic will be to go from understanding the missiological nature of the church and our call to have cultural influence (Genesis 1:28) to applying the biblical worldview to public policy. This will mean that apostolic leaders will have to hold the newspaper in one hand and the Bible in the other. We will have to do the grunt work of engaging the culture and not just having worldview conversations with other Christians. We need to go from merely speaking about being salt and light to the world to engaging culture in the marketplace of ideas. After all, since the Bible speaks truth to every realm of society, we should expect to have the best ideas and lead in a democratic meritocracy (and in oppressive structures as well).

This is nothing new for biblical leaders as we understand the divine callings of people like Joseph, Daniel, Nehemiah and Esther who applied biblical principles and the revealed will of God to public policy.

Regarding culture, although we believe in the separation of church and state we do not believe in the separation of God and state. (Although the Bible teaches that five separate spheres have their own jurisdiction--self-government, family, business, politics, and the church--each one should submit to the Law-Word of God.) Every culture was made by God to submit to His moral law codified in the Ten Commandments. (Culture comes from the word "cult" which means religion, thus all cultures were originally created to reflect the will of their creator God.)

In our thinking we must have as a goal establishing nations that submit to commandments 5-10, dealing with how humans function with other human beings in a pluralistic society (in which the free marketplace of ideas is allowed in terms of morality and religion), but ultimately some god or morality will have to create the meta-narrative of the country. I believe that all nations (Christian or non-Christian) ultimately deal with commandments 1-4, not just 5-10. (The current religion propagated in the public schools of North America and Western Europe is secular humanism, thus commandments 1-4 center around subjective pleasure and situational ethics instead of transcendent law.) Civic leaders can do this principally by favoring the God of Scripture in its civil laws dealing with religion without forcing conversions and replicating the mistakes of the past. This will be the discussion of another generation because presently we are still trying to get nations to obey the moral laws dealing with human relations (Commandments 5-10, Exodus 20).

So to summarize this section, the way towards a biblical law in a pluralistic society is to establish commandments 5-10 and use that to segue into establishing commandments 1-4, without the past abuses that included forced conversions and persecution. (Also, the New Testament eradicates and or modifies the penalties for disobeying many of the O.T. moral laws regarding sexual sin and rebellion against parents.)This can be done by favoring the God of Scripture in regards to allowing prayer, creationism and the Bible to be taught in public school, Old Testament law again becoming the template that lawyers, judges and legislators use to enact public policy, and possibly even some form of Sabbath laws forbidding certain activity on Sunday that would compete with or impede Sunday church attendance.

About the author:

Joseph Mattera is in demand internationally as a speaker and consultant. His mission is to influence leaders who influence nations. To order one of his five books or to subscribe to his weekly newsletter go to www.josephmattera.org. Joseph Mattera's list of other published books are Ruling in the Gates, Kingdom Revolution, Kingdom Awakening, Walk in Generational Blessings and Travail to Prevail: A Key to Experiencing the Heart of God. Connect with him on Facebook, Instagram or Twitter.

Made in the USA
Middletown, DE
06 May 2015